ALL YOU
LONELY
PEOPLE

ALL YOU
LOVELY
PEOPLE

Other books by John Killinger

ALL YOU LONELY PEOPLE

ALL YOU LOVELY PEOPLE

JOHN KILLINGER

WORD BOOKS, Publisher

WACO, TEXAS

ALL YOU LONELY PEOPLE
ALL YOU LOVELY PEOPLE

FOR ALL THE MEMBERS
OF THE THURSDAY NIGHT GROUP
WHO WERE
FOR THE SPACE OF SEVERAL MONTHS
THE BODY OF CHRIST
TO ME

FOREWORD

At the time I began keeping this journal I had no intention of publishing it. Quite frankly, I had no idea that the group would really go any place, much less that my little diary of events or nonevents would ever be publishable.

I suppose I really started it as a kind of therapy. I wanted to set down my own feelings of isolation in order to get a hard look at them and maybe figure out what I could do about them. The journal was to be a kind of case history, so to speak —**my** case history.

Along the way somewhere I began to entertain the notion that the notes I was keeping might be worth sharing with other people who were lonely and who wanted to start a similar sharing group in their own church or community. I thought they might profit from seeing actual transcripts of what happened in one such group, and learning what seemed to work in that group and what obviously didn't work. I spoke to Floyd Thatcher, the vice president and executive editor of Word Books, about it, and he appeared to be excited by the idea.

Then the group dissolved. I looked over what I had written, and there wasn't any plot. We hadn't achieved any great spiritual victory. Nothing seemed to build or go anywhere. All I had was a series of notes and impressions, written down over a period of six months, without any major theme or structure.

I laid the material aside. Maybe I would come back to it sometime and maybe I wouldn't. I was quite busy with other matters.

But something kept nagging at my mind. Maybe there **was** a theme running through the notes after all. It had something to do with being lonely, being isolated, being out of communication. I was working on a manuscript on communication. Again and again I found myself recalling this or that incident from the meeting of our group. What went on there was relevant; I was convinced of it. The insights were too important to me now not to be relevant to some other people too. But a book with no point, with no order, with no suspense, with no climax . . .

Finally, after an interval of several months, I sat down with the pages I had written. Fortunately I had typed them—my handwriting would probably have been irretrievable at this point. Why not, I thought, do an overlay on this material, the way singers sometimes do, going back and singing or talking over the recordings they have already made? I could break in at any point I wanted with comments on what was said or done in the group, in effect saying, "Here, this is an insight that might be important to somebody." Then I could simply spell out the insight for what it was worth and go on to the next segment of notes.

Maybe it was important that what I had wasn't really a success story. It could be that the last thing some of us are looking for today is another glibly told account of how somebody made it and made it big. That only makes us feel bad when we don't make it ourselves. Maybe a story that just tells it as it is, without any attempt to coerce the facts or make

them come out a certain way, has more meaning for us because it is more like our own stories.

So I went back through the diary and added the sections
that are indented. Perhaps, I thought, some group of people
who are starting out just as we started will want to sit around
with copies of our sessions before them and talk about what
we did. The indented portions may help them derive greater
benefit from what transpired in our midst and enable them
to proceed with observations of their own about what was
happening to us and what is happening to them. Some of the
insights became a part of the way we operated, but some of
them occurred only in reviewing the material. Writing them
down in this way is a kind of economy, an attempt to preserve
them from being lost to the reader as they were sometimes
lost to us.

The names of persons in our group have been changed to
protect identities and confidences, although I am not sure
this would have been necessary from their point of view. I
considered the possibility of releasing the book anonymously
or under a pseudonym, thus guarding my wife's identity as
well as my own. But I discussed the matter with my wife and
we decided together that the disclosures the book makes are
a kind of public confession we actually desire to make, taking
whatever consequences are due.

When the idea of publishing the journal first came into
my head, I envisioned duplicating the manuscript and sharing
it first with all the members of our group, so that they could
react and suggest whatever changes or revisions they wished.
Now, at this distance of time from the group's collapse, and
with several members having moved away, such a plan does
not seem feasible.

I can only apologize to all of them, individually and cor-
porately, for any distortions or misunderstandings that have
entered the script. I know there are many. No individual, with

his own peculiar hangups and ways of seeing things, is capable of the kind of panoramic attention necessary to view everything from its several angles, much less of the detachment required for reporting what is seen with both honesty and perspective. And I have confessed at the outset the particular problems and pressures which would inevitably affect my own interpretations.

Perhaps this only corroborates what I have taken to be the underlying motif of the entire narrative—the fundamental loneliness of human existence and the difficulty people have in relating to one another in meaningful and lasting ways. We are born into isolation and separateness. Maybe that is why the Freudians tell us we are always screaming to get back to the womb. Every man's experience is his own, and however hard we try, learning to share it with others is something we never finally and ultimately accomplish. We only approximate it, sharing now here, now there, but never wrapping the matter up once and for all.

This journal, if it has any worth at all, records an occasional instance when two or more people shared each other's lives and got inside each other's experience for a moment. The relationships were not permanent; relationships never are. But their essence, for the moments they existed, was distilled into our memories and became a part of our lives for ever.

It is hoped that the reader will discover the essence too, and that having discovered it he will be more adept than before at recognizing the fleeting but vitally significant relationships in his own life.

Life, I am convinced, is a daisy chain of these fragile relationships.

1

I am beginning this journal on a note of optimism. I feel optimistic about it today. Last night was an experience I had been hungering for. It may not last. It may not work out. But now, at least, I feel a surge of confidence. Now I have hopes that I have found what I was starving for.

Anne and I have lived in this city a little more than five years. In that time, we have not found a church where we really feel at home. We have attended many services of worship and talked to countless persons, always looking for something but never quite able to zero in on it. We joined one church soon after we came to town, but never achieved a feeling of really belonging there. Anne finally joined a church of another denomination because she liked the choir and was asked to take charge of the junior choir for a year. I encouraged her to do it, and the children and I went along with her. For a while I sort of hoped I would want to move my membership there too, but the desire never became strong enough. The people were friendly, in a polite sort of way, but it rarely went further than that. We never got over feeling that we were outsiders.

The whole thing is complicated by the fact that I am—or

have been—a minister. I have never held a full-time pastorate, but I was ordained and installed as a student pastor when I was only eighteen years old, and I served small churches for nine years while I was in college and graduate school. I always expected to have a church of my own, as ministers say, and the question of finding a satisfying group fellowship didn't even occur to me in those days. I merely assumed that I would go on working at the center of a Christian group just as I had in those small churches. Apparently Anne assumed the same thing.

But then we got derailed. I went to divinity school in the Northeast. When we were ready to come back south to the denomination I had been ordained in, I had no connections for getting a church. Eager to come back, and expecting that it was only a matter of time before I would be recognized and invited to a pastorate, I accepted a teaching post in a denominational college.

At the end of two years, I didn't seem any closer to a church than I had been before. I had become de facto dean of the chapel at the college, which gave me a wonderful outlet for my desire to preach and lead in worship. And I had been invited to become the minister of one little church which for several reasons did not appeal to me or meet my needs. But neither Anne nor I had found a church where the patterns of worship were both aesthetically and spiritually fulfilling to us.

We didn't know it at the time, but it was the beginning of a long and generally depleting pilgrimage. Before it was over, we would wonder very seriously whether the trouble was in us and not in the churches where we couldn't find satisfaction. We would even weep at our sense of desperation.

While we were still at the college, I was invited by a very famous professor of preaching whom I had admired for several years to come and be his assistant at a school in the East where he was just beginning a second teaching career. At that time I was hung up on the image of the minister as a performer, a kind of aerial artist who does a breathtaking act in front of an audience. The thought that I could improve my act was irresistible.

I don't remember thinking twice about going. My wife and I had just had our first child. At the end of the school year I was elected most popular professor on the campus and had the school annual dedicated to me for what had happened to the chapel programs during the year. But, following my will-o'-the-wisp, we packed our things and moved off to the East, confident that what we were searching for was just around the corner.

When we turned the corner, however, what we saw was pretty much like where we had been. I did become the part-time minister of a new church in a town about twenty miles from where we were living, and we formed a few friendships there that have been undying through the years since. But we were still separated by the distance from the neighborhoods where those people lived, and our lives didn't really intertwine—except in a couple of cases—the way we would have hoped for. I didn't learn much from the professor I had gone to study with, and, partly because of my diffidence at crashing in on his private existence, we shared much less together than I had hoped we would. At the end of two years I accepted an invitation to become the academic dean of an adventurous new liberal arts college in the middle of the country, and we moved again.

I didn't realize until we had left the little church back there how much even the limited contacts and feeling of group involvement had meant to me. Anne and I became rather typical suburbanites in a metropolitan area, and for the first time had a taste of the real loneliness and remoteness of that existence. Our neighbors were friendly enough along the back fence or when we met in the streets, but they wasted no time

informing us that they didn't want any more social involve-
ments. That meant no intimate friendships. It was difficult to
have intimate associations at the college too. No matter how
much you try, you can't eliminate all the curtains between
yourself and the people who work under you or over you;
they have a way of becoming evident at the most disappoint-
ing times.

In a way, my move to that position was really pathetic.
People who looked at it from the outside saw it as moving up
in the world. Many of my former associates envied me. I had
just turned thirty. I had a good position, a salary nearly twice
that of professors I had formerly worked with, and a chance
to travel all over the country on an almost limitless expense
account. Anne and I bought our first home, a lovely little
brick house in an elegantly planned subdivision. We had our
second child, another son, who was born shortly after we
arrived in our new city. I had just published my second book,
and was receiving speaking invitations all over the country as
a result of it. Things couldn't have looked rosier from the
outside.

But we were beginning to feel our first real stretches of
desperation. I had agreed to take the academic post partly
because my denomination had a prominent seminary in the
same city, and I saw it as a chance to become closely ac-
quainted with the teachers there and perhaps move into a
church position of some kind. Slowly, however, it began to
dawn on me that nobody saw me as a churchman. To everybody else I was an aggressive young academician. I published,
I spoke with ease before all kinds of audiences, I knew a wide
range of people. Maybe they saw me as a kind of apologist
for the faith, a border man. But no one saw me as what I
wanted so much to be, a churchman who felt more at home
in the pulpit and in the counseling office than anywhere else.
Academic life bored me. It had always bored me when I was

in school, and it has often bored me as a professor. But I seemed condemned to be an academician.

Consequently, when I had a chance to come to my present job in a divinity school, I jumped at it. Too hard. I took a 40 percent cut in salary and a big reduction in general situation to come to a position that would surely proclaim by its nature my interest in the church and its message and work. At least, Anne and I said, we would have friends again without worrying whether they were only being kind to us in hopes of a promotion or a raise in salary. And we would have time for each other again, which had become something of a problem in the administrative role. We were entertaining or being entertained several nights a week and were constantly on the go.

Little did we know. We moved to this city at the end of June, to allow plenty of time for community adjustments, getting situated in a church, and tooling up for the classroom in the fall. Not once, between the day we moved in and the beginning of school in September, did anyone from the school I had come to either telephone or call on us in person. A nightmare of emptiness had begun. The only friend we had was the real estate woman who had sold us our house. Our neighbors were polite and friendly enough, but nothing developed between us. We joined the church, but nothing came of that. It would be better in the fall, we said. Then things would "get back to normal."

In the fall, we hit the line. Anne began to invite people in for dinner. There were invitations in response, and a few where we hadn't invited first. But no real intimacy developed with anyone. Conversation always remained at a polite and functional stage. People never dropped in unannounced, and we didn't feel that our dropping in that way would be welcomed.

It soon became clear, moreover, that I had come into a situation where people who taught the so-called "practical" subjects related to the church—preaching, counseling, worship, Christian education, and the like—were generally regarded as second-class citizens who were only tolerated in the environs of the "real" scholars, the ones in the older formal disciplines of history and theology and biblical studies. Actually we were neither fish nor fowl. The churches and laymen were suspicious of us for being in an academic setting at all, and the professors in the other disciplines were suspicious of us because we were dealing with amorphous and subacademic subject matters. I was on my way to feeling sicker than I had ever dreamed I could.

Maybe sickness isn't the right word for it. But after a long period of isolation and loneliness, you begin to wonder if you aren't sick. You wonder how other people can appear to function so well and be so happy. Something must be wrong with you.

Anne and I have to admit this possibility in our case. Otherwise we would despair ultimately and say that the world is impossible, that relationships are impossible. We think we have tried to be loving and giving to the people around us. But we haven't felt any response. We're alone. Therefore it has got to be us or the world around us. We prefer to think it is us. At least that way we can go on living, and hope for a cure.

I have nearly given up thoughts of becoming a minister. At least I have rejected them from my conscious mind. Subconsciously, I know, I probably won't ever quit dreaming about it.

But for all essential purposes I have become an outcast in my own denomination. That is another sad story, particularly coming as it did during this period of relative estrangement and difficulty.

It happened at a time when I had just begun to be invited to a few of the more significant denominational meetings to speak or participate in conferences. The setting was at a young people's conference on the campus of a seminary on the West Coast. I had been asked to give two addresses on the subject "Christianity in a World in Revolution." The first I entitled after the assigned subject; the second was "Christianity **Is** a Revolution." In the latter address I tried to deal with the nature of Christian freedom—how Christ has delivered us from bondage to legalism and orthodoxy, so that we are now responsible centers of creativity and renewal in the world.

In the course of this address I made perhaps 45 seconds' worth of parenthetical remarks about the high control needs manifested by the official boards and agencies of the denomination. Denominational employees, I indicated, were not free to put the stamp of their individual personalities upon their work. At least they were not free to do so unless their personalities had become caricatures of official policy and direction.

Young people in the denomination, I said, should be aware of the pressures to conformity in religious circles. They should practice their Christian freedom in such imaginative ways as to communicate it to the very heart of denominational life and bring freedom and spontaneity to it.

I was totally unprepared for the explosion which these remarks generated. It was almost as if I had detonated an atomic reaction.

The president of the seminary followed me on the podium and awkwardly and blusteringly tried to refute my "insinuations." The next day he attempted to get his faculty to sign a statement disavowing any support of my sentiments. Wisely, some of them refused. The editor of the denominational paper in the state was more easily swayed. He printed the president's statement and wrote a vicious editorial in the paper denouncing me as an "immoral" person. Not once did either of them cite anything I had said. For all that unsuspecting readers knew, I was the virtual reincarnation of Bluebeard or Jack the Ripper. Other punitive actions followed within the denomination. Speaking invitations were withdrawn; or, more precisely, my name simply did not appear on the programs of some affairs I had been engaged to address; officials consistently showed a reluctance to express our disaffiliation in writing.

Through it all, the students and many of the adults at the conference responded magnanimously. They wrote many letters of protest to the editor, who they thought had defamed me, and defended not only my right to say what I had said but the truth of what I had said as well. One faculty member at the seminary resigned from his post as a result of it all.

Still, it was a tremendous shock to me. I suppose I had been naïve and idealistic, and had not appreciated the extent to which hard political factors exercise rigid control in ecclesiastical matters. I think I knew it in my mind, but I had not felt it deep down where it hurts. Similar things had happened to other people I had known. But now I was "it," I was in the center of the ring.

Since that occasion, I have lived as a black sheep in my denomination. People simply assume that I am against my church and what it stands for. I am conscious of having been admired by many persons for this. Students and younger ministers especially want to make heroes of those who exhibit any sense of independence or honesty in the life of the church.

But it is still a lonely kind of existence.

Several times, since those events, I have considered the possibility of joining another denomination. But somehow I didn't feel right about doing it. I had been in this one too long; it was part of the way I looked at things. And, besides, I knew that other denominations have their problems too. I would simply relinquish any dreams I had of participating in mainline denominational events.

I realize now, looking at the pages I have written about this, how deeply the whole matter has affected me. I have been hurt by what I think is the injustice in it. I feel like a victim, and victims become cynical. They even have a kind of pride in being victims, as though it made them special in some way.

I live with that pride. I don't like to admit it, but I do. Secretly, it is part of my problem.

Maybe my pride is what made me always feel like an outsider in the churches I attended. I was often contemptuous of what went on in those churches—the shoddy teaching in the church schools, the shabby music and prayers in the services, the incompetent preaching, the unimaginative excuses for missionary activity. Sometimes I would even become nauseous during a worship service, and have to get up and leave. I blamed the general state of the church, but now I see that a lot of the trouble was inside me. I was sick—so sick I thought everybody else was sick.

Then came last night. As I said, I am optimistic about what happened last night. I have to be. It is like a miracle drug for a dying man. It may not save me. I may be too far gone, or I may have a horrible reaction to it. But for now I have to believe in it.

2

Last night Anne and I attended an impromptu meeting of a group of people who belong to a church we have been going to for the past three or four weeks. We didn't know what to expect. It was a big chance. We knew only a very few persons in the church. We didn't know the couple in whose house the meeting was to be held. We belonged to another denomination—two others, in fact, as my wife had joined the other church I mentioned. But the pastor of this new church, Barney Hopkins, had come to see us on Wednesday evening, just after we finished supper. We liked him, and were excited about what he did with the worship hour on Sundays. He didn't know what would happen at the meeting, but he was going. We had said to him that we would try to come.

We almost backed out. Maybe we were scared, or maybe we thought it was futile. But then we were also a little desperate. So we got a babysitter and went. We found the street and located the house. There were several cars parked outside. As we went up the sidewalk behind two or three other persons, Anne said, "Let's go," and turned as if to leave. I took her arm and said, "Come on."

The couple who lived in the house had just moved in. They

had not had time to unpack most of the boxes. Things were still in disarray. There weren't enough chairs in the living room for everyone. Anne and another girl, whose name we learned was Eve Rittenhouse, had worn slacks, and they sat on the floor. I shared a piano bench with Adele Hofman, who, it turned out, was one of the two couples, with her husband Dick, who had announced the meeting. Barney was there, and his wife.

All in all, there were about twenty-five people in the room. Most of them were dressed very casually. Three or four were over forty, but the majority were clearly in their thirties or late twenties. Mostly they were couples. There were a couple of women, maybe three, whose husbands were unable to come, and one girl whose husband had died of cancer a few months ago.

Dan and Judy Quillian, the other couple who had called the meeting and the ones in whose home we were gathered, started circulating a paper to get everyone's name. But the group protested that it did not wish to do anything that formal. Eventually everyone signed the paper, but it was discarded when the evening was over.

Dan began the evening by saying that he and Judy and the Hofmans had thought of starting a group like this to meet some of their own needs. They didn't know what the group ought to do or how it ought to proceed—that was up to the group—but they had called it together. Dan said he had a problem: he found it hard to live a Christian life. As an attorney with a large legal firm, he is with people constantly in his work, but he can't get close to them. There is only one elder member of the firm with whom he feels any sense of intimacy at all. He said that he feels "tempted" all the time—he did not specify in what way—and that he has been unable to lead the kind of life he wants to lead.

Other persons in the room began to voice similar feelings.

The formal church services were not meeting their needs. Several expressed a sense of loneliness they felt when they were in church.

One of the women who had come alone, Margaret Kenan, whose husband is a doctor and medical professor, spoke of how she had felt the last Sunday, which was Worldwide Communion Sunday. She had been alone in the service because her husband was a deacon serving the communion. She felt terribly isolated, she said. Then another woman moved over and sat by her in order to share communion with her. Afterwards, the woman had thanked her and said how much it meant to her to be able to have communion with her.

"**She** thanked **me**," said Margaret, "and it meant so much to **me**!"

One young woman, Rachel Anstruther, urged Eve to tell about her parents' experience. Eve described the experience very articulately, in such a manner as to let you know, if you didn't already, that she is a very sharp gal with a no-nonsense approach to things.

Her father and mother had never been very close to each other or to her, she said, or at least had never seemed to be very intimate. As a family, they had lived pretty much in isolation from other people. Eve had never had friends to her home; she had never felt welcome to do so. Her parents had never had neighbors or friends in either. Only a few times, she said, they had had some elderly ladies in for dinner, because they knew the ladies were in no position to return the favor and get something started.

Then, about six months ago, her parents had become part of an unusual church in their city—a church which consists entirely of small cells or units of twelve persons each and meets only in the cells. Every time a new group of twelve is formed, that group is sealed. The persons in these small groups really get to know each other well. It wasn't long before her father was confessing to his group how he felt threatened by other persons, and how he compensated for these feelings by trying to dominate others. If he tried to dominate this group, they weren't bothered by it. He felt enough security to tell them how he felt.

Eve had just recently had a telephone call from her father. He and her mother had had their entire group into their home for the whole weekend. Eve was astonished. She couldn't believe it was her father telling her these things. He was talking to her more intimately than he ever had before, and was able to verbalize how he felt about her. He loved her, he told her.

"I can't wait to go home," she said. "It's like I had a whole new set of parents I never knew before."

Barney Hopkins had entered the conversation at one point, and Eve had said to him that she felt certain hostilities toward him as her minister. He fingered the neck of his sport shirt and said he would like to talk to her about them. He wanted to be accepted in the group as a human being, he said; he had needs too. Others admitted having some difficulty at this point. He was their minister, and it was hard for them to accept him outside that role. Obviously one need the group ought to meet would be this one: people could voice their hostile feelings to one another in a supportive context, and perhaps work through them.

At one point Barney turned to me and asked if I would express to the group what I had said to him the evening before regarding my feelings about the worship services of the church. He felt that something encouraging ought to be voiced to balance the conversation, which had seemed to be extremely negative on the subject of formal worship. I repeated essentially what I had said to him the night before, that I was so excited by the services that I felt as if I were being lifted by the hair of my head. I went on to say how lonely Anne and I had been in this city, and how desperate we had felt for this kind of personal sharing and intimacy. Afterwards, several people confessed that they had been threatened by my presence as a minister and professor until I had spoken of our needs. Then they could accept me as a person like themselves. I did feel that there was a place for both, I said, for the small group like this and then for the more formal experience of worship; I thought the formal experience would be heightened in meaning because of the intimacy gained in the small group.

Anne didn't say anything. She said afterwards that she wanted to join in several times but that my being there inhibited her. She let me say it for us.

One woman, Alma Ryder, stated flatly several times that she didn't feel the need for this kind of group. She worked in an insurance company, was open to everyone she met, and felt that people shared themselves with her wherever she was; any more intimacy was simply superfluous to her. There was perhaps more friction around her remarks than around any others of the evening. Two or three of those present wanted to know why she had come, then. She said she didn't know what it would be like. She couldn't understand the hunger that most of the people seemed to feel. Life was just different for her.

There was a great deal of debate about what form the group should take on subsequent occasions. Some felt that we should divide into smaller groups for more intimate conversations. Others felt that it was too soon to divide, that some of us didn't even know all the members of the larger group yet.

Dick Hofman, who was sitting in a rocking chair near the door and seemed to exude a kind of benevolent-father air over the proceedings, obviously wanted things to move in the direction of more piety, with prayers and maybe even Bible study. Eve did not hesitate to express her disdain for this kind of approach. I had to confess that I too was turned off by the thoughts of that. I don't know why it bothered me. Maybe because it reminded me of college prayer meetings I had attended, where there was usually a lot more heat than light.

It was finally decided that we would meet the following week at the Quillians' again, and let things take their course, depending on who were there and what they wanted to do.

Anne and I were the last ones out of the Quillian house. We were excited by what we felt there, and wanted to chat as long as we could. We are both gregarious by nature. But it was more than that. Maybe we thought it couldn't last, and we wanted to savor it as long as we could.

I hope it will last for a while at least. I feel something today I haven't felt for a long, long time. I hesitate to call it hope, and yet that's what I think it is. For a change, I have the feeling that life isn't over, that it isn't finished and rounded off. Something seems to be opening. It reminds me of those scenes in Samuel Beckett's play **Endgame** where the characters are nearly at the end of everything and they think they see a louse or a rodent or something and are afraid the whole mad game of life will get started up again. I see something beginning, only I am excited by it. Maybe life **will** get started up again.

I've had a funny feeling this week. Every time I've passed the building where Dick Hofman works, I've wanted to stop by to see him. I feel very close to him. Somehow his piety doesn't turn me off. It must be real with him. I want to be with him. I want us to share our presence with each other.

It has been a different sort of week. The aura of that meeting last Thursday night has cast its spell on everything. It began that very night. Anne had had a sinus infection that had settled in her bronchial tubes, and she had been disturbed for several nights with a hacking cough. Lying down seemed to start it up again, and she found it hard to sleep. I never said anything about it, for I knew how it bothered her, but I was inwardly annoyed by it, as I too had difficulty sleeping when she began a coughing spasm. But that night I felt more positive. In fact, I felt so positive that I noticed the way I felt; it obviously contrasted with what I was accustomed to feeling. I felt very solicitous about her comfort. I reached over and put an arm around her several times during the night. I wanted her to feel okay. It didn't matter if I was disturbed; I didn't need the sleep. I felt great!

All week I've had this super feeling, like a feeling of confidence or joy or something I can't quite describe. I know I've been more positive in my attitudes toward my colleagues and my students. I can accept a lot of the little picky, unimportant things we do just to keep the machinery turning around the school. The whole atmosphere seems healthier to me. And I know it is I who have changed, not the place itself. I feel different, somehow—stronger, happier, more flexible. Maybe even younger.

I have to go on a trip this week, and will miss the second meeting of the group. I'm sorry about that, almost. That is, I wish I could be there, but I don't feel any diminution of confidence because I won't. It's sort of comforting, in fact, to realize it will go on. Anne is planning to be there and has promised to tell me everything that happens.

I feel that I can make my trip and fulfill my engagement better **because** the group is meeting. I know it sounds funny, but it seems important that the group be together, even though I can't be there. Normally I hate to travel. The last couple of years, I have begun to have these fatalistic sensations whenever I have to be separated from Anne and the boys. I've tried to struggle with them and overcome them, to rationalize them and see them for what they are. That doesn't help much, though; I still feel kind of empty and sick in my stomach whenever I have to leave. I get so lonely. But I have a feeling I can make it fine this time. Something buoys me up. I feel like my old self.

3

The trip was a good one. I hate to be sophomoric and say, "Gee, I feel great," but that is really how I feel. It was a denominational meeting for pastors and leaders of suburban churches, sponsored by one of the more liberal elements in our denomination. Could it be more than coincidence that I was there just at this time? I had prepared a paper on new patterns of worship in suburban churches, and was to participate in one section of the conference dealing with that topic. Then, on the last evening of the conference, I was asked to lead a worship service and preach.

I had decided some time ago not to preach a traditional sermon. It seemed to me that the same old approach to group worship on the last night would simply undo whatever progress had been made during the week toward transcending the old patterns of life and work in the church. But I admit I was a bit uneasy about how what I had planned would work. Maybe I was a little bit insane. I had this gnawing feeling that I was building up to some kind of climax where everybody would know I was at the point of a breakdown.

I was very nervous the first day or two. A false kind of religiosity seemed to hang in the very air we breathed. Sometimes I wanted to shout out an obscenity and see what would happen. My group leader for the conference invited several of us to his room for a briefing session. He puffed on a cigar and he and another pastor from Mississippi talked about how they were fighting the good fight against the rednecks in their churches—how they took a little here, gave a little there, and so on, managing to eke out a pretty good living for themselves and their families in the process.

God! I thought. I'm going to puke! I can't stand this! This is nightmarish, it's . . . it's . . . it's Kafkaesque!

I called home the second day to say, "Anne, I don't know if I can make it or not. It clogs my pores. I can't breathe."

My section of the conference was particularly intolerable to me at first. There were about a dozen persons in it. Four or five were pastors of churches. Only one of them had an advanced theological degree. One man was a denominational editorial writer who had once taught at a seminary. The one woman in the group was an elderly employee of the agency sponsoring the conference. Other participants were students in theological seminaries. Another was a denominational worker in some role I can't remember, who was there for the week to play the piano in the assembly meetings. Not one person except myself, I was certain from the outset, had ever read a single important volume on the subject of worship; yet we were there to fashion a paper on worship which theoretically would be put in the hands of every member in the denomination.

To my amazement, however, I began to feel more comfortable with them. Two or three of them I genuinely liked. I found myself even becoming more tolerable of their ineptness for our task. I saw how tendentious and radical my own position paper on worship would probably look to the average grass-roots Christian, and how important it was to moderate the theories and tone of my statement before it went out as a broadside. In the end, I was the one who proposed that the denominational editorialist do the final drafting job on our group's ideas—even though two or three of the students in the group had complained to me privately that he would outfit it in such plain prose that no one would even bother to read it. I felt that they were wrong, and that the man operated as he did partly out of a sense of love for those with whom he must communicate.

On the next to last night of the conference, each group was to have its own private vespers. We had agreed to follow our group leader's suggestion that we have ours in absolute silence. No one would speak a word. We climbed the hill to our little retreat place and entered a room where the chairs were set around a table. On the table were some rolls from the dinner table, a pitcher of water, and a single glass. There was also a transistorized radio tuned to a nearby rock-and-roll station and playing softly.

We sat around the table, listening to the patter of the disc jockey and the ironic words of the songs. The leader removed his shoes and set them under the table. We all followed suit. He motioned to the lady in our group, and she stood up, stepped over to the table, poured a bit of water in the glass, drank it, pinched off a part of a roll, ate it, and sat down. We went around the circle, and each did the same in turn. Then the leader put up his hands to the person next to him, and that person put his hands up against the leader's.

"Peace," said the leader.

"Peace," said the other. And so on around the group.

Then we put on our shoes, turned off the radio, and went out.

It is impossible to describe what I felt—what I think we all felt—that evening. We had been an uneven group. We had disagreed about many things. We had probably been threat-

ened by each other. But now we were one. I think we would
have done **anything** for each other.

Now I am not saying I felt this way because of the Thursday
night group. I might have felt it anyway. I have felt such closeness before. But somehow there was a link between Thursday
night and this. I felt as if I had discovered a kind of substratum
in the Thursday night thing, something that would underwrite
this conference experience and keep it from existing as a
mere isolated incident. The joy spots in my life were beginning to join up, to make a web, so that I felt a relationship
among them. They would be able to sustain each other and
wouldn't fade so quickly.

One of the things I was able to admit to myself during the
conference was the envy I had felt in the past for certain
ministers in glamorous churches. One of them was speaking
at the conference. He was minister of an active suburban
church in one of the finest cities in the country. I had known
of the church through its previous minister. How is it, I had
often asked myself on earlier occasions, that a guy like that
carries off a position like that, which I would give my eye
teeth for, and I have to settle for the isolation of a teaching
position?

But this time it was different. I saw this particular minister
struggling with his own growth problems. I listened as he
tried to communicate with the people at the conference, and
heard the innuendoes, the faint whispers under the words he
was actually saying. I felt his own terrific ego-needs, and I
tried to answer some of these. I enjoyed his presence. I was
glad I didn't live in his shoes. I was glad I lived in mine. I was
able to celebrate the variety and excitement of our common
life, and to thank God for who I was and where I was and how
I did my thing.

By the time we got to the last evening, I was less worried

about what I had planned to do for the worship service. Somehow I had more confidence in the people attending than I had had; they would **make** it work.

Ed Summerlin, a wonderful jazz musician from Pleasant Valley, New York, had flown in for the occasion. Ed is a saxophonist who has written a lot of exciting new music for Christians. We asked a combo from a nearby seminary to come down and form his backdrop. That night, Ed and his combo played a prelude. Then we sang a couple of his songs. Then Larry Matthews, a minister from Virginia, led us in our public confession.

After some more songs, we had a scripture reading. Ten fellows, standing helter-skelter around the room, read ten different passages simultaneously. It was wild. I watched the reactions, some of pain, some of intrigue, a few of actual bliss. Gradually the readings trailed off until a lone voice, that of Jim Slatton, a tall, mournful-looking Texan, was the only one continuing. Jim said afterwards he thought we had set him up for that.

Some people were genuinely puzzled by the procedure. Others said that they first regarded it as a parody of our usual practice of reading scripture. Then, as they concentrated on the reader nearest them, they began to hear with strange new powers of hearing.

After some more songs, it was time for the sermon. I said I wasn't going to preach. I talked for a couple of minutes about how most of us had gotten in the habit of "dispensing" sermons, prayers, and other God-effects, and how it had dulled us to the real spiritual life around us. I suggested that we needed to put off all our professionalism for the evening, and just be people. I asked the group to break ranks, so to speak, and rearrange their chairs in small circles of eight to ten. Then I asked them, if they felt like doing it, to touch their neighbors. Most of them did.

"Now," I said, "if you feel like it, say what it is that is bothering you most in life—maybe it's a feeling of inadequacy, or a fear of not succeeding, or poor relationships in your family, or some other thing that you haven't even faced or articulated before now in your own mind. This is the body of Christ. Maybe you can say it here."

This was the moment I had been afraid of. It could have died right here. I thought for a few seconds it was going to. There was silence in the big room. Then someone started whispering in a circle on my left. Then someone else in a circle near the back of the room. Then the whole room seemed to burst into low-voiced conversations. I walked back to where Ed was sitting on a piano bench, and he and I talked about things personal to us.

After five or six minutes, I asked the groups to break off talking for a minute so we could play a little game. I instructed them to take turns standing in the middle of their groups and being passed around from person to person, beginning with the last person who had spoken. Their feet were to remain in the center, so that the bulk of their weight was actually on the floor. But they would have the sensation of being handled and supported by their groups.

It was fun to watch them as they did it. Some of them clasped their arms together and shut their eyes and just sort of rolled around the group, being held up and passed from person to person. Three or four persons in one group near the door, I am told, did not like this, and walked out; the ones remaining in their group moved over and joined another group nearby.

Next I asked them to be seated again and do one more sharing act. "You've shared your pains and problems," I said, "but the body of Christ is more than that. It is also a sharing of strengths and hopes, beliefs and excitements. What is one thing that really means a lot to you, that keeps you going when nothing else does? What has meant most to you the past two or three days? Can you tell that to your friends now?" Also I said that we ought to be doing something symbolic while we were sharing these items. I had wanted to have a communion service, but my denomination still has a few members who insist that only the strict membership of a local church is entitled to have communion together, and the officials who were responsible for the conference had demurred at the suggestion that we break bread together. So Larry Matthews and I had filled a lot of paper bowls with salted peanuts and raisins. We passed these out to each of the groups, and I suggested that they might feed each other some nuts and raisins as they talked, remembering that we feed on Christ daily and that our sharing this way is also a kind of feeding on Christ. Instantly the place was abuzz: they had much to talk about!

Finally, when this was done, I asked them to observe a minute of silence in which they were to do anything they felt like doing. I hadn't planned this originally, but they were all carrying the ball so well, I decided they ought to have a moment for invention. Some began reaching out to touch each other again. Some embraced. One or two fell to their knees. One group on my left held hands all the way around the circle, stood up, raised their hands high overhead, and softly began to sing the doxology. Slowly the others joined in, until everyone in the room was participating. It was the most beautiful doxology I ever heard—a cappella, slow, soft, and completely sincere. Talk about a climax! Where do you go from there?

Ed led us in some more songs—nobody seemed to want to quit. People moved around freely, shaking hands, embracing, patting shoulders, talking, singing, keeping time to the music. It was an ecstatic experience.

What it did for me personally was to underline the reliability of the congregation in worship. There were a lot of gaps in the service I planned. In fact, I was scared and embarrassed at having such a sketchy order of service to go by. It could have been nothing! But it wasn't, because they filled in the gaps. They had a chance to give themselves in the service, and they did it. They preached the sermon each of them needed to hear. I had few illusions about it. I knew that most of the ministers there would go back to the humdrum routines on Sunday morning. But I had a feeling that that evening would haunt them for a long time, and maybe it would inspire some of them to have some confidence in their own congregations, and to take the risk I had taken.

Driving home, I knew I had been affirmed too, and in a way different from the way I am affirmed when I preach a regular sermon. People often praise what I have said when I preach. But this time they were happy about what **they** had done. I could enjoy it without being in the limelight. It was a good feeling. I felt close to God.

I have since discovered that numerous groups around the country are using similar methods to revitalize corporate worship. The spotlight is turned off the minister and the choir and onto the people themselves, who are urged to cluster with their neighbors and share how they are feeling about things. Sometimes they are asked to talk about a passage of scripture or something that has just been done in the liturgy. Other times they are requested to talk about their needs, affections, and experiences of grace. Often the cluster arrangement is used for small prayer meetings in which individuals are encouraged to pray for one another by name.

The overall effect is to rehumanize worship. This is important, for worship has tended through the years to become fixed and abstract, with too little attention paid to the particularities of personal existence. If the Christian faith is an incarnational faith—that is, if it is based on the belief that God took an important step with us by becoming incarnate or enfleshed in Jesus—then we can never get enough particularities into the picture. We must strive constantly to plow them in, so to speak, and enrich the soil of our common experience.

I must admit, too, that I have occasionally had a negative reaction at this very point. It is possible for this act of exchange to degenerate into a kind of parroting of the pious thing to say, without any more sense of sweaty reality about it than there is about more abstract and impersonal liturgies. Participants say what they think they ought to say under the circumstances, or what they think the others in the group want them to say. They hesitate to express dissenting opinions or feelings of distaste or actual revulsion.

It seems to be a temptation for people to resort to pious language on such occasions, when what they probably ought to do is to secularize their statements as radically as possible, bringing the world of affairs into the sanctuary in all of the latter's angularity and brokenness. Too many "Praise the Lords" or "Glory to His names" may be a tipoff to the kind of phoniness that tends to haunt the Christian experience in the world. Some gut-level language and honesty, on the other hand, may indicate a truer commitment to the struggle for genuine illumination.

For additional information on personalizing worship, see Lyman Coleman's books **Discovery** and **Serendipity,** published by Creative Resources, Word, Inc. (Waco, Texas), or write to Ben Johnson, Director of the Institute of Church Renewal (1610 LaVista Road N.E., Atlanta, Georgia). I have also included a chapter on "Persons" in my book on new worship, **Leave It to the Spirit,** published by Harper & Row (New York).

Anne's report of the Thursday night group was not entirely

positive. There was a lot of dissension, she said, about the direction the group should take. The arguments were basically those of the previous meeting.

Experimentally, those present had broken into smaller units and gone into separate rooms for the remainder of the evening.

Anne had been put in a group composed primarily of young mothers whose most pressing needs were related to their manner of child-rearing. She said she had talked entirely too much, but had ended by playing the mother-figure to the girls. She is an extremely acute individual and had shared insights they were grateful to have. But she had felt that she was entirely on the giving end, and that no one was interested in her problems, which were mostly of another order. Afterwards she expressed this to Barney Hopkins.

"You think you've got problems!" he said. "You should've been in my group; all we talked about was the Girl Scouts!"

This week was not so good. I had to make another trip, this time to a western state where I was the speaker for a city-wide Festival of Faith. In the mornings I spoke in the chapel of the local seminary, and at night in an ecumenical church gathering. The settings were just the opposite of the encounter experience we had had that evening at the conference: hideous old church sanctuary, timid little choirs singing hopelessly archaic hymns, and tired ministers praying trite prayers and making equally trite appeals for "a good offering." I preached. I did the performer thing, the thing I had set myself against. And people were kind and complimented me for doing it. But somehow I felt that I had slipped into the past again, that this was a throwback, an atavism. This was the way it used to be done. We couldn't go on doing it this way. The church had to catch fire again, had to become personal again. People had to feel the Spirit again.

I particularly noticed the absence of young people. They

were obviously turned off by this "old-people's church." I
couldn't blame them. One night I almost went to sleep in the
big leather chair behind the pulpit while I was waiting for my
turn on the program. I must have stifled a dozen yawns.
The seminary chapel was a little better, but there again we
were locked into a terribly traditional approach: call to worship, hymn, scripture, prayer, sermon. I thought, what a rotten
job we are doing educating young ministers and church
leaders! Even in the seminary we lack the insight or the motivation to change our approach and stimulate the students
to do something different. Christianity like that is such a bore!

One of the few bright spots in the week was a visit from
Michael Rhodes, a very intelligent, articulate Presbyterian
minister from a little town in Oklahoma. Mike drove over on
Tuesday morning and stayed with me until after lunch on
Wednesday. I first ran into Mike when he was president of the
Student Fellowship at Southwestern Baptist Theological Seminary in Fort Worth, Texas, where he sometimes got into
trouble with the campus hierarchy because of his free and
imaginative ways. He has grown more in the five or six years
since he left seminary than most men grow in a lifetime. I
think Mike has a rare talent with language. I don't know if it
ever comes out in the pulpit or anywhere else, but it comes
out in his letters. They are always full of word play, which,
when it is good, is the surest sign of a dynamic, interesting
person.

Mike and I talked a lot about the church and the ministry.
He is not so keen on small group encounters as I am. He said
he had been to one such conference recently with about
four hundred ministers and their wives. The thing that bothered him most was the way the leaders demonstrated how
encounter sessions are supposed to work. "I **really** love you.
I **honestly** and **truly** do. I want you to know that. I **really** care
for you." Too many adverbs, said Mike; they made him think

it was phony. If these people really loved each other, they didn't have to make such a point of it, they would know it. I'm not sure; I don't think we verbalize such sentiments enough. But I did see his point.

"Shout out the first word that comes to your mind," they instructed the groups at one point. "I said an obscenity," said Mike, "but I didn't say it loud enough."

Another time he told a dirty joke. The groups had been going at it for a whole day, and he had just sat silent through it all. This was another shortcoming, he felt; some people manipulated the groups with their own problems while others fell into long stretches of withdrawal and quietness. That night, one minister's wife who had done her share of talking throughout complained that they weren't really communicating with each other. She pointed to Mike and said, "Why, I don't even know that man over there; he hasn't said a word." Mike figured this was his cue. He was tired of it all. So he stood up and told a very funny story, which he related to me, about pubic hair. The minister's wife immediately jumped up and left the room. The next day she returned to Mike and apologized. She had really liked the story, she said, but was shocked to hear it in such a context. Mike figured she was hung up on sex.

The point was, he said, the groups weren't really doing anything to work through the basic life-styles and problems of the participants; they always stopped short of illumination, or got tangled up in the matter of confession itself. I could follow his reasoning, but I wanted to reserve judgment. I was still living out of the overflow from the Thursday night meeting I had attended.

I was scheduled to fly to New York from the western engagement on Thursday to attend a professional meeting, but the airline was inoperable because of a strike and I used the excuse to fly directly home. That way I would be able to attend the group meeting that evening, and also attend a dinner on Sunday night with some people I had met at the church.

Dan and Judy were having their house painted, so we met at another home in the suburbs. Several couples had other engagements that evening and didn't make it to the group. Eve was in the hospital for minor surgery. There was some carryover of persons from the first meeting, and there were some new faces too. Normally I would have been very tired, having just returned from a couple of weeks away, but my sense of expectancy had kept me buoyed up. I went to the meeting with a feeling of eagerness.

Maybe I was too eager, or maybe I was tireder than I knew, but nothing much seemed to happen. There was some rehashing of what had happened in the small groups the week before, and there was a great deal of talk again about whether we needed to break up into smaller units. Dick and Adele Hofman helped to save the evening, I thought, by telling about their weekend, which they had spent in a lay renewal meeting in a church in Mississippi. Apparently they do this sort of thing rather often. They want to have such a meeting at our church, but don't seem to be able to generate enough enthusiasm for it in the session to get it officially on the books.

Finally several persons shared with the group some of the highlights of their week. Rachel Anstruther told how the previous week's discussion of young parents and their children had helped her to be a more loving mother during the week. Adele said that the encouragement of the group had helped her to relate positively to a neighbor whom she had never liked. Ellen Harris told of going up to a stranger in a store and complimenting her on her pretty dress.

"You must have known I needed a lift today," the woman said.

Someone mentioned the local school situation, which led

to some confessions of racial prejudice. Dick and Adele
Hofman said that they had had no qualms about moving into
a fringe neighborhood, but that they were having a real
problem accepting the possibility that their daughter might
be bused to a predominantly Negro school if a rezoning
ordinance took effect. Dick admitted that the fear of violence
was the thing that scared him. He had always cringed from
physical threats of any kind, he said. Adele had grown up as
an M.K. (missionary kid) in a country where whites were in
the minority, and might be expected to approve a similar
situation for her daughter. But it was a great worry, she said.

One thing led to another, and the discussion got onto the
subject of what the average suburban church member can
do to get over his feeling of isolation from inner-city problems, so, if for no other reason, he will not be so deathly
afraid of situations like the one the Hofmans are faced with.

Marnie Jones, whose husband Cecil is an account executive
for an advertising company and was out of town on business,
suddenly and unexpectedly became the star of the show. She
displayed a tremendous knowledge of inner-city opportuni-
ties—the kinds of organizations and situations where any
concerned citizen can become involved in the lives and problems of people not fortunate enough to live in the suburbs.

It became apparent that most of us do not use our imaginations enough or do not have adequate motivation really to
become involved in political and social matters in our own
community. I realized what a cocoon of rationalization and
sophistry I am always weaving around myself, insulating myself from the cost and demand of actual Good Samaritanism.

Dick Hofman suggested that we close the evening with a
minute of quiet prayer, with time for anyone who felt like
doing so to voice his own petition. "Lord, help me to be
better," someone prayed almost at once. There were two or
three other prayers made audibly. I didn't feel like adding

one. I still wasn't comfortable with this kind of pious con-
clusion. Neither was Anne. But I knew I loved Dick Hofman.
Later in the week Anne said, "You really feel close to the
Hofmans, don't you?"

"Yes," I responded.

"So do I," she said.

What Anne and I have both noticed is a new feeling of
peace and fullness we have not felt for very long at any time
before. Suddenly we see our world in bloom and know we
live in paradise. Not a sickly romantic, always-subdued-light-
and-evergreen kind of paradise, but one full of all the potential we need for our existence the rest of our lives. I have quit
yearning for faraway posts and places. I begin to understand
the meaning of the pregnant now. I realize that I have lived
for the last twenty years as a kind of escapist, refusing to wrest
the substance out of where I was at any given time by always
envisioning the way it was going to be when I got to somewhere else at some other time. I know this sounds amazingly
simple, and it is. But I had not, in all those years, really faced
up to my problem. It is almost as if I had suspended living for
that period. Not really, of course; it has been a rather full life.
But I now see them as immature years, years partially wasted
because of my ambition to be somewhere else.

Could a real Christian fellowship make all of this difference? I now see that Anne and I have not had such an intimate and sustained fellowship since we were both young
people growing up in the church. We have been wandering
through the world in search of many things—maturity, responsibility, engagement—and had actually forgotten the importance of continuing to be sustained by such a fellowship. Now
our lives are taking up nutriment from their roots again. I
hope it lasts.

4

What a blow the last meeting was!

It began innocently enough, with chitchat about this and that, and then with Adele Hofman's setting up a big, floppy cardboard box decorated with different words and colors on each side. On one side, in cheerful colors, were words like "Enlightenment," "Me," "Engagement," "Mine," with a vacant spot in the middle. On the opposite side, in equally bright and cheerful colors, were words like "Concern," "Love," "Listen," "See," "Feel," with the word "God" in the center. The third side was done in black and white and gray. The word "God" was in the center, flanked on either side by the word "Polarity"; then, in rectangles all over the remainder of the space, were haunting words from daily newspapers: "War," "Hunger," "Poverty," "Strike," "Demonstration," etc. I did not see the fourth side.

I thought it was interesting that several of the girls became immediately engaged in a very careful analysis of the meaning of each side. Obviously it was important to them to solve the riddle of the artist's message. Dan Quillian and Bill Duval finally said they couldn't see anything in any of it; Dan pre-

43

ferred getting the box out of the room where it wouldn't obstruct his view of persons across from him. Abruptly, Dan began a new tack. He recognized a serious problem in his life as a Christian, he said: he lacked spontaneity. He could often think of something he should have done for someone after it was too late to do it. For example, he cited, there was an alcoholic court stenographer whom he saw occasionally and had seen earlier that day. His firm could not employ her very often, for she was extremely unreliable. As soon as she had done a little work, she would press her employer for some money, buy something to drink, and then disappear to her hotel and be unavailable for an unspecified period of time. Or she might appear drunk at a trial and miss valuable sections of testimony. Dan wanted to help her. He felt that inviting her to a meal that evening and giving her some genuine companionship might be more important than going home to a cozy meal with his wife and then coming to the meeting. But he couldn't do it. He saw himself doing one thing ideally but another thing functionally.

Or, as another example, he remembered an occasion when he had wanted to give Dick Hofman a $400 guitar he owned. Dick could play it and Dan couldn't. But he didn't have the courage to do the generous thing. He could see himself making the magnificent gesture, but couldn't follow through on it. This really bothered him, he said; he longed to be a more instantaneous person.

As he talked, I could not help thinking of Camus' **The Fall,** with its underlying thesis that the real symbol of man's loss of innocence is the ability to see himself making poor decisions or failing to act on his impulses. The seeing is the damnable thing. Until we see ourselves failing, we are not really aware of fallenness.

I also thought of something I had read once about the fear

of falling, and how all kinds of falling are really connected—falling from great heights, falling into sexual situations, falling into degradation, falling into improper speech, falling in love, falling in business. It is a curious thing that a person who is free of the fear of falling in any of its guises is probably free from the fear in all its other guises. A person who hangs loose sexually is less likely to be afraid of airplanes or business failure, for example, while a "tight" person is afraid of all three areas. Is the whole matter of grace related to this? When we have enough confidence in the grace of God, does it free us from all the fears of falling? I suspected that it might be true of Dan that inwardly he was not entirely reliant on this sense of grace. He talked on other occasions as if he were, but I wondered.

My own reveries were interrupted by Judy, Dan's wife, who said something about trusting in God and not worrying so much. Somebody who knew Judy well, I think it was Vernon Harris, said, "Something really happened to you in Memphis, didn't it, Judy? I remember when you came back. You were really different." Memphis was a reference to a Faith at Work conference she and her husband had attended several months ago.

"Yes," said Judy, "it really did. I'll give you an example. I was never able to get along at all with my mother-in-law. Dan and I started going together when I was fourteen and married when I was nineteen. We've been married now for seven years. And his mother has never accepted me. It doesn't help that we live just two blocks from them. She's always dropping in.

"Well, I tried for a while just doing whatever she said. I was polite and gave in to every suggestion. But I really hated her and hated myself for knuckling under that way. Finally, after I was at Memphis, I had the courage to tell her to go to hell. And then, when I couldn't stand things in that arrangement either, I said to God, 'God, I'm giving it all over to you. You help me. I'm not going to rely on my own strength anymore.' And he took over. I know he did. We began to have more of a working relationship. It isn't perfect, by any means, but it's something. And God did it, I know he did."

Rachel Anstruther said she wished it were that way between her and her three-year-old. Maybe God would help her the same way. She believed that she wouldn't have had a child if it wasn't meant for her to be able to raise the child well, but she was truly miserable most of the time. She felt like such a failure.

At this point I interjected a speech. My voice sounded weak and funny to me. I had tried to practice silence at the gatherings because I didn't want to intimidate anybody with my theological background. It wasn't easy, because I frequently had the urge to pontificate on this matter or that. Many of the problems and queries seemed so elementary to me. As Anne and I agreed in private, we had long ago hashed out most of the things that appeared to be of primary concern to most of the participants. Maybe we had always been too analytical. But now, hearing myself talking, I felt that I was faltering.

I told Rachel about having recently heard a sociologist speak who had spent a year in Syria. He had commented on the difference between the way the Syrian parents approach the matter of child-rearing and the way we approach it.

"Over there," he said, "a father may give one of his children a few sheep. Then he will encourage another child to get them away from him. Trickery, stealing, any method is okay. If the child succeeds, the father mercilessly beats the child who lost them. Now compare that kind of education for life with the kind we give our children. We do just the opposite. And we produce men and women who don't know how to be individualists anymore."

What I wanted Rachel to see was that she need not feel so

guilty about having to oppose her child so much; it might be good for the child; maybe the child was going to turn into a marvelously aggressive person.

Perhaps we don't understand the mechanics of grace, I suggested. We worry so much about everything. Worrying interferes with our ability to enjoy life. I alluded to Judy's experience with her mother-in-law, and how she had felt better and was able to have a more honest relationship with her when she finally gave up and quit trying. When she got rid of her anxieties, I said, she was able to use her real resources.

And here is where I got in trouble. I wasn't trying to provoke anyone. In fact, I didn't know what I had done until it was done. But I said that the important thing was getting rid of anxieties so that our real potential could emerge to meet situations. It doesn't matter how, I said, whether you assign them to God or put them in the box we had sitting here a few minutes ago. When we can transfer our anxieties to somewhere else, we feel free to cope with things.

The fat was in the fire! Adele started to say something, but Judy interrupted her.

"Just a minute, Adele," she said, "I can't let what John said go unchallenged. I don't agree that we can put our anxieties in a box and everything will be all right. I know that God did what was done between me and my mother-in-law. I didn't do it. I couldn't do it. I told God it was up to him, and he took care of it. I am convinced of that, and I don't like to hear anything like you have suggested, that the box would have worked as well."

Dan was right there too, sputtering to get into the conversation. His voice was raised and he was clearly passionate. He didn't agree that one could put his anxieties aside that way and have things turn out any better. God had done it, and that was all there was to it.

Margaret Kenan was sitting beside Dan. She is a doctor's
wife, and it surprised me to hear her agreeing with Dan. She
looked disturbed.

There was a flurry of conversation, with people all around
the room trying to be heard.

Anne raised her voice above the others. "Just a minute,"
she was almost shouting. "Just a minute! You people don't
listen. You get all hung up on words. You're twisting what my
husband was saying. It's just like the other night, when I said
that a psychologist had once told me I had to push the button
to kill my mother* before I could have a good relationship
with her. You got so excited about the word 'kill' and kept
talking about it and talking about it. Now you can't get off
the word 'box'."

I said nothing more. I had not meant to start a conflagra-
tion, and now that it was raging I didn't know how to stop it,
short of saying, "Wait, that isn't what I meant at all."

The trouble was, I thought maybe they had heard me cor-
rectly. Anne's defense aside, maybe they had pounced on the
crucial issue. I did believe that it would have done as much
for Judy to have put her anxieties in the box as it did for her
to give them up to God. God had not changed things with
her mother-in-law; as a matter of fact, the relationship didn't
sound all that rosy to me anyway. She had simply transferred
her worry about her mother-in-law to a reservoir called God,
and then she felt relaxed enough to handle the situation more
adroitly. I firmly believed that.

While the conversation went on animatedly around me,

---

*This was not really so harsh as it appears in print. Anne's allusion
was to a problem she had always felt, as the youngest of several
children, in meeting the expectations and winning the affections of
her mother. The psychologist's point was that she must in effect
"destroy" the false image she had of her mother and accept her real
mother on a simpler basis.

then, I sat there wondering what prayer and faith really do mean. I wondered if I wasn't in the wrong place after all. I didn't want to destroy their simple faith. But, on the other hand, I was not prepared to say, "Oh yes, God does everything for us if we put matters in his care."

People kept talking about my remarks and reacting to them. Sometimes they openly disagreed with them. Other times they tried to interpret them charitably. Once even Dan said that perhaps I was trying to jab them into thinking about the matter and had used a technique he sometimes used in the courtroom, of posing something hypothetically and then not going on with it any further—as if, had I gone further, I would have necessarily spoken their own conclusions on the matter.

But I didn't rise to the bait, if it was bait. Inside me, I had resigned the matter for the evening. As I told Anne afterwards, I had two choices: I could retire, or I could crush them with theological questions they couldn't answer. I had no desire to crush them; I even felt guilty for having upset them the way I had.

The meeting broke up rather abruptly. Dan was in command. He ended a speech by saying it was time to release the babysitters and by standing up and leaving the sofa where he had been sitting. Everyone followed suit. I had the feeling I had just been spun out on a revolving door and was on the outside, away from everybody.

We chatted in little clusters as we were leaving, but the group soon dispersed. I had the feeling that a lot of people had been threatened, particularly because the box thing had come from a clergyman. Three or four persons to whom I would normally have said goodbye slipped out without my getting to speak to them.

Outside in the chilly autumn evening, Anne and I said goodnight to Judy while Dan was talking to Bill Duval some distance away. He came over as Bill drove away and sug-

gested that we remember Bill in our prayers that night; he
had just told Dan that he had had a real experience, one he
had been looking for for a long time.
   I felt very peculiar. Surely Bill's experience had had something to do with Dan and Judy's testimony about God's power
to do everything for them. And, if that was so, then I was
devil's advocate; I was the secularist, standing in the way of
such an experience.
   I was really mixed up. I felt a little sick inside. I didn't feel
wrong; everything in my own experience told me that my
views were all right. But I had this crazy feeling that everybody else believed something else and that they had to feel
all right in spite of me. I was a hindrance to them.
   William Schutz says in **Joy** that there are three basic human
needs: inclusion, control, and affection. My first two had been
shot all to pieces that night, and the third was met negatively
instead of positively. Distrust, that is, seemed more predom-
inant than love. I wondered if there were some there who had
remained silent but would have agreed with me. I wished Eve
Rittenhouse had been there. I knew how she would have felt.
I was really low. I wondered if the end had not come into
view.
   Anne said on the way home that Barney Hopkins had said
to her in the hallway, "Now don't let this get you down. You
come on back next week." She had told him it took more
than that. I knew that it did, too, but I wondered if we would
show up a couple of more times and then ease off, just to
preserve us from the appearance of being quitters. I had grave
doubts about the compatibility of the group. Most of them
were as sensitive on religious matters as the fundamentalists
in my own background, and I had been burned by the
fundamentalists.
   It is now Monday, though, and the funny thing is that I
have felt better and better about what happened. I felt awful

that night, and I didn't sleep well. I tossed a lot and had feelings of anxiety, because I knew I genuinely cared whether we could go on in the group. The next day we made a trip home because my wife's uncle had died, and I felt blah all day about the night before and wanted to shut it out of my consciousness. But by Saturday I was beginning to feel better. I seemed to feel that the human relationships in the group were stronger than the religious disagreements. Maybe I'm wrong, but I hope not.

As I've reflected on the matter, I have conceded that there is a part of me that often lives with the same naïve kind of faith Judy and Dan were championing. In fact, I have felt this way increasingly since attending the meeting on Thursday nights. I know that when my life is affirmed by friends and loved ones, I have this sense of the presence of God, and I talk easily to him about the most casual matters of the day. Maybe what I am really looking for is this simple, celebrative kind of faith-relationship. I don't expect to give up my psychological understandings of how I function and how other people function in the world; but maybe they will be subsumed under a kind of positive, less reflective way of living and moving.

I began a short term of teaching in the church school yesterday, and several persons from the group were present for the class and seemed eager for what I had to say. I saw Dan later in the coffee hour, and he expressed a desire to be in the class too, though he is prevented by his own teaching duties. Maybe he meant it. At any rate, my positive feelings were reinforced, and I didn't sense that I had been unconsciously rejected by the group. I think something will come out of last week's confrontation—maybe something good. I am looking forward to this week's meeting.

I was right about it. Last night was tremendous. I am beginning to believe there is a periodicity about these things, that we oscillate from our most barren and apparently unproductive sessions to our richest ones—and maybe back again. We really turned some kind of corner last week, because things happened during the week. Liz Delacorte more or less pitched the ball out last night by telling what had happened to her. When Dan talked about the alcoholic court reporter at the last session, she found her point of contact, for she was a former alcoholic herself. The next day she telephoned Judy and asked if she could come over and talk. She took half a day off from work, and she and Judy drank coffee and talked. What she told Judy was essentially what she summarized for us about her experiences as an alcoholic. She thought she could help Dan with the woman he was concerned about, and wanted to know if she could talk to Dan too and tell him her story.

That night when Dan had finished dinner he called Liz and she came back over and stayed until after midnight. When she went home, she was singing to herself. Her sister, who had heard her come in, said to her the next day, "You told somebody about yourself, didn't you?" She had, and she was happy.

Liz is in her late thirties, and unmarried. She is an attractive person and speaks with a beautifully full, well-modulated voice. I don't know yet what demons have lived inside her, but apparently they almost controlled her at one time. She has gone the whole route—AA, therapy groups, psychiatry, the whole bit. AA helped her to stop drinking. She had her third "birthday" a few months ago. She also joined the church a few months ago. Barney Hopkins told her he thought she had something to give, and that she ought to throw in with the group at his church. This appeal reached her, because she did have something. She hadn't dreamed then of a group like this one, where people became so intimate about things. But the church had not met her loneliness problem, and, when the group was announced, she moved instinctively toward it. I asked Liz in what way she felt that this group was different for her from AA. She said she felt free here to talk about God, and that was important to her. When she had made her third-birthday speech at AA she had told about joining the church and what God meant to her, and some of the persons there had felt very uneasy because of this. She was not criticizing AA; she just felt restricted there from talking about this meaningful aspect of her life.

She was obviously worried about how her announcement to the group would be met. This was the first time she had really opened up and talked at any of the meetings. She had often experienced rejection, she said. Once she bared her feelings at a therapy session, there was a silence, then somebody cracked a joke and the whole group turned to another subject. It was hell. She was taking a chance in a church group, she felt, telling her story. But you could feel the love and compassion in the room; it just sort of oozed out to her from every direction. Most of us, I know, didn't see her demon as being any fiercer than ours. Maybe we even felt that she had been pretty lucky that it had taken such an objective form, and she could at least partially measure her recovery in objective terms, namely, whether she stayed off the bottle.

When she concluded her revelation, she made a kind of apology for having taken the center stage for so long, and said how important it was for her not to feel rejected by the group. She would try not to bring her trivia to the group, she said, but this was extremely important to her.

John Rittenhouse, who had come to the meeting in a bright red shirt and matching striped trousers, said what I thought was the right word for all of us to hear at that moment. "But I want you to tell me your trivia," he said, "because I get to

know you through the trivia. I want to feel that I can trust you
with my trivia, and not feel that it will turn you off."
    The whole question of participation was open before us
now. Rita Denny, who had been a silent guest, an eavesdrop-
per, from the first, said that she didn't think she trusted the
group enough to reveal anything very central to her. Rita is
a petite girl, maybe middle twenties. I don't know if she is
married or not. She had a few close friends, she said, to whom
she would divulge very personal things; but she didn't think
she could tell these things here. She had come to the group at
first thinking it would be a Bible study group or something
like that.
    The question of trust became focal; participation depended
on that. I don't know whether Anne spoke up or someone
asked her a question, but she indicated that she had felt
dropped by the group after the remark about killing her
mother. Several persons responded briefly; it had been an
important remark to them, apparently, and one that had made
Anne interesting to them as they reflected on it. Still, they did
not pursue the matter of her feelings now, and she sank back
again, burrowing into her hole. I felt sorry for her and wanted
to say, "Come on, tell these people what agony you are in,"
but I didn't.
    One reason I didn't was that I knew there were others there
who also had huge feelings of rejection. One of them, I felt,
was Dick Hofman. I almost said this, but didn't. What right
did I have to open other people's wounds? I might be wrong.
    Then Dick said it, right out of the blue. He felt rejected
from the first.
    I could have cried. "Dick," I told him, "I almost said some-
thing about that a minute ago. I wish now I had."
    And suddenly I found myself "explaining" Dick's rejection
to him and everybody else; somehow it seemed crucial to me

in the whole chemistry of the group. It was even related to my own feelings of rejection that week before. I told how I had felt after the "box" incident. I felt handicapped in the encounter, I said, by my theological training and professional experience; I knew I could demolish Judy and Dan's arguments, from a logical standpoint at least, but I didn't feel that that would be fair. Besides, I didn't want to do or say anything that would diminish what they were feeling. I wasn't against what they were feeling. But I just seemed to find myself in a position under attack, and couldn't really come back at them, so I felt excluded.

"I want you to know what this group means to me," I said. "I feel as if I have picked up living with a group of Christians in a way that I haven't lived with people in nearly twenty years. I don't want to be here as a professional Christian; I want to operate out of my weaknesses. That way I'll share who I really am with you, and you can either accept or reject that.

"Now I'll try to say what relation I think this has to Dick's sense of exclusion. I feel a deep, underlying sense of relationship to Dick, something that has drawn me to him from the first. But he and I operate from different poles when it comes to talking about our faith. He and Judy and Dan talk one way, and I talk another. I came out of an extremely conservative church and I am still reacting against that. But I feel rejected on the other extreme just the way Dick does on his. And I want him to know that I love him and don't want him to be different."

Eve Rittenhouse said that she was sorry, but she did want Dick and Adele both to be different. They turned her off with their pious language and their wanting to have public prayer and all that. Adele was almost in tears, and I'm sure Dick was too. It was really out in the open now. The hostilities, the feelings of exclusion, the antipathies—we were knee deep before we knew it, and going deeper all the time. Dick and Adele's way of talking seemed to be a big issue. Eve and John had lived in a missionary situation for two years in a South American country, and they were fed up with what they regarded as hypocritical, pietistic types. They said that the first time they met the Hofmans the Hofmans said, "Oh, you must know our friend so-and-so, he has meant so much to us," and that they had almost puked because they did know the person and felt a passionate reaction to him. They felt there was a phoniness about his religious talk. Now it was the Hofman's vocabulary that they found too full of big, fluffy pieces of piety.

I felt like the man in the middle. I really appreciated the Rittenhouses, I said. I had wished, the week before, for Eve's presence; I had wanted her to jump in on the "box" discussion and say the things I didn't feel it would be fair for me to say; I felt that I could trust her to say how I felt. But, on the other hand, I understood what the Hofmans were saying with their Jesus-talk. I had reacted to such language over the years because I had not heard it used always by people who were sincere or whose lives were pledged to back up the way they talked. But now, I said, I found that the Hofmans were reinstating that language for me; it seemed more natural to me, coming from them.

What I was also trying to say between the lines, probably, was that I thought Eve and John were being too hard on Dick and Adele because they were reacting against their own backgrounds. When they had worked their way through their own hangups and antagonisms, they too might be able to talk the language of Zion again without having violent reactions to it.

But I wasn't the only person in the middle. Judy Quillian said it made her feel like a hypocrite or something, because she was a close friend to both the Rittenhouses and the Hofmans. Rachel Anstruther said essentially the same thing. Something wonderful was happening to the group. It was happening to Eve. She said to Adele, "Maybe I feel better about you now. I think I could discuss with you what it is that puts me off about you. I don't think I could have done that before."

Adele was pleading: "Oh, do help me."

I couldn't help feeling that the Hofmans had gotten a lot of stuff thrown at them that they didn't deserve, that they were sort of innocently in the middle with a lot of people who had worse hangups than they. Even Barney Hopkins had said to them that he thought they were a lot less tight and stiff than when they came to town a few years earlier. "You were going to save the world then," Barney reminded them.

I wondered if Barney, as a minister, was not threatened a little by their idealism. Afterwards I realized that I was. I have always been threatened by extremely religious types. Their dedication reminds me of the fervor of my own commitment at one time, and I feel guilty. I can usually rationalize my way out of it, but I know I am rationalizing.

Still, it was a beautiful moment. Feelings had been poured out that had been dammed up for years. Differences had been expressed and, to some extent, resolved. They had not been eliminated, but now they were out in the open and they weren't so horrendous or insuperable as they had probably seemed to us before. Most important of all, we felt united; there was an atmosphere of joy and excitement in the room.

The time had been forgotten, and most of us were long overdue to get babysitters home. Now we were pleasantly exhausted, and the evening seemed to have run its course. We felt good and relaxed, and fell into spasmodic small talk.

Finally I said, "I don't think Dick ought to be the one to have to suggest this tonight. I feel like holding hands and having prayer before we go." Apparently almost everyone felt that way too. Hands reached out instantly, and we bowed our heads. I was almost weeping for joy. "Lord, thanks for people," I said. "Thanks for **these** people, and for their support."

Ellen Harris, next to me, said a brief prayer. So did someone else. Then I was surprised to hear Eve pray. Then Adele prayed. Dick didn't. I'm sure he wanted to, but this was his way of making a concession this time.

Finally, when everyone had had a chance to say a prayer if he wanted to, and there was a long silence, I said, "Well that's it, Lord. Thanks."

Dick and Adele were sitting on a sofa with Liz. Immediately three or four persons rushed from across the room and tried to hug them. When I looked, two girls were on their knees in front of Adele. Then, in a few minutes, Adele went across to sit beside Eve, and the two of them talked.

The men gathered around Dick. When I went out in the hall and Dick and I were alone with Vernon Harris, who was our host for the evening, I took Dick's hand and said, "Dick, I love you."

"I love you too, John," he said, and we folded our arms around each other and hugged in genuine affection.

Afterwards, I felt bad that we hadn't turned to Vernon and hugged him too. He had been quiet all evening. I wondered if we had not failed him miserably, all the way through.

We had failed Anne. She said so when we got into the car. She had been left hanging again, she said. She had confessed that she felt rejected, and still nothing had happened. People had absorbed the confession and gone on.

What did I think about it? she wanted to know.

I knew how she felt, I said. But maybe she hadn't gone

into detail enough to give the group anything really to work on. Liz had really spilled her guts, and there was something there to deal with. We could affirm Liz for who she was. "That's what John Rittenhouse said," she replied. "He said I should have been more selfish, and demanded some attention. He knew what I was feeling, and reached over and held my hand once. Then afterwards, when Barney was talking to me and asking if I didn't have something left on my agenda, John was sitting there with his hand on the back of the chair, gently rubbing my back."

I had the feeling that next week would be her time, that it would come off for her as it had for me tonight. She was low now, but her frustrations would work her into real projection the next time.

Looking back, I am more convinced than ever of the cruciality in human relationships of revealing enough of one's self for others to relate to. How many times people fail to pick up on something we say merely because we haven't said enough for them to know where to begin. Untrained in counseling methods, they do not ordinarily pick up clues easily and ask the questions which might draw us out. Inwardly flustered, they pass on to something else in the conversation, and we are left with our sense of rejection.

It is a vicious circle. We tend to release only small, tightly compressed bits of ourselves because we are uncomfortable in our relationships. The more uncomfortable we are, the briefer and more tightly packed these "signals" are. We have held in and repressed the urge to speak so long that when we do dare to utter something it bolts forth awkwardly and unnaturally. We are frightened at the sound of our own voices, for we know we aren't coming through in our normal tones. Then, when others don't respond to who we really are, but to the false noises we have made—or when they don't respond at all—we become even more knotted up inside and have an even harder time speaking the next time.

Liz, in her self-revelation, could almost be termed a compulsive confessee. She talked as if she had to talk or die, as if she had to say everything there was to say about herself or she would simply explode. When she had finished, however, she had so thoroughly exposed herself to the group that nearly everyone in the room felt comfortable with her and wanted to support her.

Anne and I, on the other hand, had been so selective in our manner of self-exposure that people had not really felt they knew us when we were finished. They knew that our communications were not the whole story, that they were signals we had sent out which must be decoded and unpacked for their wider meanings. Maybe Liz, through her several associations with encounter groups and therapy sessions, as well as through Alcoholics Anonymous, had reached a stage in her ability to communicate in the group that we had not yet achieved.

This insight—of the importance of laying enough clues in front of others for them to know us more thoroughly —is applicable in almost every area of life. Some students withhold themselves before classmates and teachers. Teachers withhold themselves from students. Ministers hide their inner lives from congregations. Businessmen hesitate to divulge their personal beings to other businessmen or to company officials. Family members even hold out on others in their families.

There is no easy way to overcome this dreadful reluctance we feel. The only cure is to take the risk of exposing the self more completely and see what happens. Not just once or twice, but many times, until exposure becomes a new way of reacting to others. Those who are most adept at it say that it is the only way to live, that once it has been experienced you are sure that it is the safest, most relaxed, and most enjoyable method of relationship there is. The more I practice getting beyond my own self-imposed defenses, the more certain I am that those people are right. Living openly is the only way to live fully in the world.

5

Today is tremblingly beautiful. The autumn sky is clear and blue, the air is fresh and warm. I was alone most of the morning, writing in my study. Anne and a friend were shopping and she didn't get home until nearly two. About noon I put on my coat and went out to walk around the yard.

I went back to the big pine tree at the boundary and found a fresh bed of brown needles under and all around it and lay down in them so I could look up at the tree and the sky.

Off in the distance, a butternut tree rose tall and colorful against the blue of the horizon, and a white jet trail intersected its lines. The old oak tree behind the house, tall and twisted like the lines of a tree in a picture in a children's book, made me feel unreal as I stared at it. The whole scene looked like an etching out of the Currier and Ives collection I examined in the bookstore a few days ago.

I felt so wonderfully warm and happy. I didn't even feel guilty about it, or think, what right have I to be happy when there are others so miserable in the world? I just basked in it, the way I was basking in the sun. My life is good, I said to myself, and I felt like weeping for joy.

Last night we went by to see Eve and John. It was an interesting evening. John is presently a traveling represent-
ative for a book company, but has resigned effective a couple
of months from now. He and Eve lived in a house in a fash-
ionable section of town but decided that things were getting
on top of them there so sold the house and moved into an
apartment. They have been deliberately trying to minimize
their material needs, and thereby to reduce their actual
spending.

I was impressed particularly by John's statement that he
had to learn to be a better parent when they entered the
apartment, because it is smaller than the house and he
could not merely retreat to another room to get away from
the children; he feels that proximity has led to the kind of
interpersonal relationships he was avoiding in his former
situation.

We were perfectly relaxed. I think all of us, at one time or
another, sat on the floor. There was a bowl of popcorn, and
cokes were offered, but there was no compulsion to have
any. We just talked. I was glad to find Eve less aggressive
than she has been on Thursday evenings.

The evening gave every promise of turning out to be
merely a pleasant couple of hours of exchanging information
about ourselves and getting to know each other better. But
then Eve said, "I don't know if it's fair to bring this up now,
Anne, and maybe you prefer not to say anything, but to
keep it for the group. But I had the feeling that you didn't
get it all out the other night."

That did it! Anne was ripe, and she split open. Lots of
stuff came out, mainly about the sense of isolation and frustration she has felt for several years. She needed women
friends, she said, and doesn't have any. Eve understood; she
doesn't have women friends either.

John and Eve both felt that Anne should attend a sensitivity training session. They had each been several times, and believed that going had changed their lives. Eve said that she had finally accepted herself as a beautiful person when she attended her first training group. She had appeared at her best physically all week—had even had her hair done and kept her makeup repaired all the time—and had apparently gotten rave treatment from some of the men in her group. This had done something important for her. She and John both spoke quite openly of their thoughts and feelings. It was the honesty of their self-regard that had first attracted me to them.

Eve said she had another man in her life whom she loved very much. She indicated that there was another woman in John's life. Each accepted this from the other, because they were agreed that there were certain things they could not do for each other, certain needs they could not fulfill, which the other persons could. They felt that they loved each other better for it.

In the climate of such openness, Anne allowed herself to think and talk more freely than she had before. She realized there were certain things she resented in me very much. One thing in particular that bothered her was that I worked at home so much; she felt that she needed the home to herself, and wished I would go to my office and stay there regular hours like other men.

John wanted to know if she felt the need for other men. She didn't think she did. One of her problems, she said, is that she is attractive to men. She would like to enjoy men's company, to talk about their businesses, their hobbies, their families, and so on, without their wanting to go to bed with her. But invariably, she said, the way men feel about her leads to the loss of their wives' friendship. Eve said it was this way with her too.

It seemed to me that both Eve and John were amazed at

the maturity Anne displayed when she finally began talking. Eve even commented on it.

I asked Eve if she envied her that. Maybe I was trying to say to Eve that I thought she was still searching for something, perhaps even her womanhood, womanhood as a full, relaxed, compassionate state of being. I wanted her to see it in Anne when it finally got out from under the wraps as I thought it had then. I thought Eve and John had done a lot for Anne, and I wanted to do something for them in return. They are wonderfully refreshing persons, but I think they are still being hard on themselves, and will be until they can relax and accept some of their past that they are still trying to reject.

The evening had a very positive effect on Anne. She got a lot out of her system and felt that Eve and John still affirmed her in spite of it. Today she says she will make it, that she is going to enjoy the great life she has, and make the most of it. Maybe for the first time, she expressed her delight in the city we live in. "It is a good place," she said, "and I am glad to be here."

She didn't understand how Eve and John could maintain affairs with other persons; her own marriage was too sacred for that, and she was very much in love with her husband. But she was not judging them; she knew that they were probably fuller persons for the course they had taken. She didn't want them to be hurt by anything. She was so happy with our children. Life began to look very, very positive to her.

Joe Marston called me to play tennis today. We drove out to his club on the edge of town. Karla has quit coming to the group. I guess she didn't need it. I don't think she did, really. She and Joe appear to have led full and well-balanced lives. It was probably just a time-consuming meeting to her.

Anne has talked for two days about the sensitivity training sessions. She doesn't want to attend one, but I guess she feels compelled to defend her decision because of the way the Rittenhouses urged her to go. She has read a good deal about such sessions. "I don't feel the need to do those things," she says.

I believe she's right. At a certain stage in some people's lives they are probably very helpful. But Anne is sensitive. What she needs is to be around people more. She thinks the group is doing this for her, and I agree.

We talked at noon about the difference between our group and various kinds of encounter sessions run by psychologists and psychiatrists. I don't think we will ever get to the level of raw intensity in our group that exists in most secular sessions; we don't seem to feel the need for that. But we do accomplish many of the same things. We touch each other a good deal, but only as a **result** of feelings and not as a **means** of producing feelings. That may be good in the long run. And I think there is an added advantage to our way of doing it. We don't have a reentry problem. Almost everybody I know who has been in sensitivity training says it is hell for a couple of weeks trying to accept the pressures of daily life when they return to their life situations. One woman feels that her experience of reentry was actually destructive to her. We don't have to reenter. We see these people at least once a week, sometimes much more often. We expect to continue to see many of them for months and maybe even years to come. When we go out from the group and fail, we come back again and report that. Then we go out and try again.

And it means something to me that we meet under the sign of the Cross, figuratively speaking. Nobody says anything about that. It isn't ever formally noted. Sometimes we don't get around to praying. But there is something supportive and meaningful about it, nevertheless. What we're attempting to do is to feel and to give compassion; and it is easier to do that, week in and week out, when you know, even subconsciously, that you've got Christ and the church behind you.

This observation has seemed truer and truer to me as I have had opportunity to observe numerous kinds of encounter or sensitivity experiences. When the experiences are almost totally secular there is frequently a kind of viciousness at work among the participants— an attempt to cut everybody down to size, to deflate the relatively well-satisfied ego, to pick at the persons who appear to be happily adjusted until they become angry or confess that they are as maladjusted as everyone else.

In the group that is even nominally Christian, however, there is something else at work. It is almost as if the participants were secretly haunted by the Fourth Gospel and the Johannine epistles, where so much is said about the love of Christ for his followers and the love they should show to their brethren as a result. This special quality of love seems to underlie everything that is said or done. At times it is felt more overtly than at other times. But it is almost always there.

I'm afraid a lot of people felt let down this week. I don't know what it was, unless it was the intensity of last week's confrontation, but many of us were in a lackadaisical mood. We didn't seem to want to engage in anything too serious or too personal. It was all right, I thought, but I worried a bit for two new persons who were in the group for the first time. One is a single woman and the other is a divorcee. I'm sure they must have felt that the evening was a rather strange and empty one.

First, everybody wanted to chat with the person or persons next to him. Noisy interchange filled the room for nearly an hour. Then, when conversation became more general, many people seemed to be feeling humorous. Exchanges went on at a casual, almost flippant, level.

Dan Quillian reported that he and his law partners had been visited during the day by an unbalanced man who appears in their offices almost every month when the moon is nearing its fullness. It seems that the man had once dated a girl and then lost her to a local policeman. After that, the man said, he was persecuted by the police. They had a machine for producing soundwaves which they beamed at his head, so that he felt vibrations in his ears whenever they turned it on. The sight of a police car was enough to send him into panic. He had visited approximately seventy law offices in an attempt to find a lawyer who would help him bring suit against the police. He had begun coming to Dan's office to get help in a suit against the various law firms which would not take his case against the police. Now, said Dan, he shows up regularly; it seems to have something to do with the phases of the moon.

This of course struck many of the group as being funny. A kind of low-grade hilarity seemed to have a grip on us. A few persons laughed almost to the point of hysteria. Any new remark struck them as funny and sent them into renewed fits of laughter.

Ellen Harris struck a serious note by saying she had come upon a real problem during the week and needed the support of the group to deal with it. She works at a hearing and speech center in a local university, and had just been assigned to tutor a deaf girl who is trying to prepare to pass a beautician's exam administered by the state. Much of the exam, said Ellen, depends upon a knowledge of human anatomy. Ellen didn't know anatomy, and didn't know much about the nature of the state exams, and so felt rather overwhelmed in her task. She thought somebody in the group might have resources which would be helpful to her in aiding the girl. Even more, she needed to express her sense of anxiety and to feel the closeness of the group as she tried to cope with it.

Still the humor persisted. Somebody else recalled knowing a girl with impaired vision who had had trouble becoming a beautician. I think it was one of the men who observed that, from the looks of some of the women he had seen emerging from beauty shops, there were "a lot of those" around. Witticisms and little gales of laughter continued to break out spontaneously around the room.

Some attitudes appeared to crystallize and reveal themselves around this mood which just seemed to hang on. Adele Hofman and Margaret Kenan said they thought it indicated the need for some structure which would "get things started" each time we came together. Adele confessed that she was very conscious of "wasted" time.

"Normally," she said, "we know we have to be home at a certain time to relieve the babysitter. I like to visit with people too, but when I'm paying a babysitter to come, I want to get down to a serious level as soon as possible."

Two or three other persons defended the way the evening had been going; they felt that laughter and frivolity were important to their lives too, and they did not feel that the time had been merely wasted.

Someone else, I think it was Dot Hopkins, suggested that we might have someone prepared each Thursday night to talk briefly on a particular topic if things didn't just get started naturally. General sentiment, however, seemed to inveigh against this; many felt that it was important for things to take their own course.

Dan Quillian said he had to confess that he was afraid of silences.

"Yes, Dan, we've noticed that," Marnie Jones said.

There was more laughter and more discussion of the merits of structured sessions versus the merits of unstructured sessions.

Judy Quillian said that when she came to the group she wanted us to have prayer together. She said she hated to say it, because it sounded like "a Dick Hofmanish thing to say," but that was how she felt.

Dick remarked that he didn't feel like praying at the moment. But a few minutes later he gallantly suggested that we follow Judy's desire and join hands for prayer.

My guess is that most of us did not feel like praying just then. But we did feel a need to shift gears for the time remaining, and even those of us who did not want to pray acquiesced in holding hands and waiting for individual prayers to be made. I honestly did not feel like offering even a silent prayer. I only listened to the ones who did speak out, and was glad to be with them.

Once, something struck me as funny and I almost laughed aloud. Anne said afterwards she had looked around and had seen the smirk on my face; she thought I was feeling pious about what was being prayed.

About half of us did not verbalize a prayer; two or three persons prayed more than once.

Somehow we got into a discussion of how much we feel that God is involved in the small events of our daily lives. Anne said, almost categorically, that she did not feel the need for addressing God directly, that it just did not occur to her. I remembered a recent instance when she thought something had happened to one of the children and I heard her say, "Oh God, don't let it be, don't let it be!" and I tried to communicate this across the room to her by a skeptical little frown. Later I was to be sorry for that.

Dick Hofman said that he prays many times during the

course of a day, and wishes he could "bother the deity" with more prayers. For example, he said, he had recently had an occasion when he could not find a discrepancy in his accounts at the office. He struggled and struggled with the ledgers. If he couldn't find the problem, no one else could. Finally he closed the books and said "God, I can't do it, you'll have to do it." Then he went home for the night.

The next morning he looked at the books again. Still the troublesome area was not apparent. Again he closed the books. In desperation, he repeated his prayer: "God, I can't do it, you'll have to do it." He shuffled a few papers on his desk. And there, like an answer out of the blue, was the item he was looking for. The crisis was over.

"But what about the times when the answer doesn't come?" asked Anne.

Dick said he didn't mean that God reached out and rearranged his papers or anything like that; God used **him** to do it; when he wasn't open to God, God simply couldn't make full use of him.

Dick's wife gave another example of how prayer worked for them. She had left the brake off in the car when she parked it in a parking lot, and the car rolled back and hit another car. When she told Dick what had happened, he said that the insurance company would raise their rate. "This really bothered me," said Adele. "I didn't want our rate to be raised. We couldn't afford it. I prayed that God would do something. Then our rate **was** raised. But God answered my prayer by enabling me to accept the raise." What she would like, she said, would be to be able to live submitted to God all the time. Yes, agreed Dick, that would be tantamount to the biblical injunction to "pray without ceasing."

Dan said that he knew people who lived open, successful lives but did not ever feel the inclination to pray or "drag God into it." Rachel Anstruther agreed; she thought that God was "anonymously present" in a lot of people's lives, so that they actually lived as close to him as others who tried to be in an attitude of prayer all the time.

Liz Delacorte said that she had often felt answers to her prayers as an alcoholic. Sometimes, she says, she gets a terrible yearning for a drink. Maybe it's four o'clock in the afternoon. She thinks, "I'm going to die if I can't get something to drink. I'll tell the boss I have to go home early for something, and I'll stop by the liquor store and get what I need." But she says, "God, help me to hang on another half hour." Then, half an hour later, still fighting the battle, she prays the same prayer again. "Oh God, just one more half hour." Then it's five o'clock and it's all over; she feels grateful and good because she didn't succumb.

Someone said, "This conversation reminds me of the one the other night when we had the box here."

"Yes," agreed someone else, "I seem to have heard all of this before."

I asked if Dick and Rachel and Dan and Liz weren't all saying essentially the same thing but in different words. They all seemed to have a sense of the meaningful presence of God in the world, and they all spoke of the importance of being open to him so as to live at high tide, so to speak. Maybe the Hofmans used the vocabulary of traditional prayer more than the others, but the effect was generally the same.

After we broke up, several persons told our visitors how glad they were the visitors were there; some apologized for the fragmented way the evening had proceeded. I think we all wondered if they would come back again. In their place, I doubt if I would.

As we pulled into our driveway, Anne exploded in resentment. "Nobody there gives a damn for how I feel about things," she said.

I couldn't believe it.

"What do you mean?" I said.

"What do you mean, 'What do you mean?' You know damn well what I mean. None of you cares what I think. Whenever I said anything, it was just tossed aside. And you **frowned** at me! You tried to put me down, all the way across the room! You tried to control me. You didn't want me to say what I thought."

I had not meant the frown that way, I said; I hadn't wanted to communicate outright disagreement with her, or to silence her, at all; I had wanted to remind her that she did sometimes pray and mean it.

She slammed the car door getting out. I could go back if I wanted, but that was her last time. That was it, finis.

I took the sitter home and came back to find Anne sitting in her rocker in the den. Her face was tense. I apologized again for what she thought my frown had meant. She lashed out at the group. She couldn't stand all that God-talk, she said; people weren't being honest. I tried to remind her that we are not all alike, and that some people are just as sincere in their God-talk as others are in their more secular way of speaking.

"Why should I accept them when they don't accept me?" she said.

"But they do accept you," I said.

"You know what I had this tremendous urge to do tonight?" she said. "I wanted to stand up right in the middle of all that talk and say 'Chickenshit!' I wanted to see their faces. I wanted to hear what they'd say after that."

"Why didn't you?" I said. "I think Cecil and Marnie and some others would have laughed and applauded. They were probably feeling the same way."

We talked about it again today. Anne is still struggling with an acceptance problem. She also confessed that she has secret fears that the group will break up, and she is reluctant to lay her innermost self bare lest she do it and that happen. "Suppose it does," I said. "Let's make the most of it while we can, and then maybe we will be well enough to start something else if it does. How long have we been meeting?" "Six weeks." "And how long has it been since we've been comfortably related to a group like this one?" "Ten years?" We sat in silence for a moment. Then she said, "I guess I'm looking for a miracle. We have to be patient."

We Westerners—especially Americans—are so pragmatic that we think we are wasting time when nothing appears to be happening. We could learn much from the Oriental, for whom waiting is considered to be an extremely vital activity. The person who is attentively waiting is preparing himself for what will come his way only because he has waited. This might be called an attitude of **creative waiting.**

Being able to handle these uneventful evenings is extremely important to both the individuals involved and the group as a whole. It should be verbalized near the beginning of any group's involvement with each other that there will be such routine times and that they should be expected. They are not wholly useless times, regardless of how dull or boring they may seem.

None of us lives at a continually high level, and neither does any group. There are periods of quiescence and gestation, during which previous events are assimilated and new outcroppings have a chance to develop. In this sense, such periods are essential. In the overall program or life of a group, they are fully as important as the times when excitement fills the air.

Today was a breakthrough for me. I've got to come up with

a book title for a new manuscript. I have eight or ten, but can't decide which is the best. So I printed them up in a list and xeroxed them, intending to share them with my seminar group and with the sharing group tonight. But I amazed myself by pulling them out and showing them to a number of faculty members through the day—at a conference, at lunch, in my office.

I know that wouldn't sound like much to anybody else, because people undoubtedly share things with their colleagues in most situations. But it was a big thing for me. I have lived for so long with the feeling that my colleagues don't care that I would not ordinarily have bothered to consult them. I feel good about having done it.

Anne did it the other night. We rocked along for a few minutes, chatting about this and that, and then she threw down the gauntlet.

"I am sick of all this God-talk," she said.

As well as I can recall what she said, it went something like this: She felt that the way some people use God-language tends to divide groups and churches into "spiritual" types and "unspiritual" types, the spiritual ones being those who use pious phrases. She herself does not feel the compulsion to mention God in every conversation or to call on him constantly in prayer; he is already **there** in her life, at the center of who she is and how she feels from day to day.

She feels that it is a travesty on the life and ministry of Jesus, who secularized the holy, to have to cast a veil of piety over everything before considering it to be properly religious. We are all so uptight, she said. She had recently attended a Women of the Church meeting, where most of the women were over fifty, and had spent part of the day rolling bandages with them.

"A lot of you," she said, "speak contemptuously of those

women because you don't think they're really spiritual. But it's just that they're relaxed and we aren't. They've found what they're looking for, and we're still frantically searching." Two or three women in the group picked this up immediately. They had attended WOC a few times, but had no interest in it at all. One of them, at least, was intrigued by Anne's obvious enjoyment of the group, and said she would like to go with her the next time and observe the group through her eyes.

It was clearly Anne's evening. What she said dominated the conversation until some of the couples had to leave. And she was pretty much alone with it, defending her point of view.

Afterwards, eight or ten persons lingered and continued to talk. I was talking to Liz and Eve most of the time, and didn't hear the conversation among the others.

As Anne reported it to me, she and Barney Hopkins argued a good bit over the God-talk issue. Barney was afraid she had hurt Dick and Adele Hofman's feelings, because they were obviously the prime users of such language. Anne kept insisting that she loved the Hofmans and that she didn't really mind their using any kind of language they wanted to, but that what did bother her was the way Barney identified them as holy people because of the way they talked and judged her to be unholy because she didn't talk the same way.

Anne was miserable the next day. Apparently Barney had convinced her that she had offended Dick and Adele, and she was worried about that. She also said that she felt like a fool—she had been the focus of attention all evening and had said things that alienated her from people and had received little support. I told her I thought tension was good for the group, that it had always been productive before, and that she should wait and see what came of it this time.

"But what if I have hurt the Hofmans?" she said.

"Call Adele if you want to," I responded, "and tell her how you feel."

About two o'clock I telephoned home to see if she was feeling okay. She and Adele were having tea. I said I would see them later.

Anne had phoned Adele and told her how awful she felt. Adele said, "Can I come over?" Dick's car was in the garage, but she borrowed a friend's car and came immediately. They had tea and cookies and talked. Anne explained to Adele again how she felt, that it wasn't anything personal but that she resented feeling marked as irreligious or unholy because she did not use overtly religious terminology in her conversations. Adele was warm and assuring.

"Dick and I were talking about it," she said, "and we think there is so much we can learn from you."

Saturday night the Hofmans and their children came over for dinner. We had a wonderful, relaxed evening by the fireside, and talked of many, many things. We all felt very close to one another.

This week we didn't meet as a group because of Thanksgiving. Several couples were going away, and we thought it would be a good experiment to see how we got along without meeting. Personally, I have missed it. It seems like a month since I have seen everybody. And things have not gone as well as usual. I'm not sure the two are related, but I suspect they are.

We did have Liz and her sister and Vernon and Ellen Harris and their children over for Thanksgiving dinner, and had a grand day. Ellen brought oysters and blueberry salad, and Anne fixed our usual turkey feast. We sat down to eat at two and didn't leave the table until nearly five. When we sat down, we all joined hands for the blessing.

"Just think," Ellen said, "if it hadn't been for the group we wouldn't be having this together."

6

None of us will soon forget last week's meeting. It will be remembered as one of the severest, hardest-hitting sessions we have had—and yet, withal, one of the most productive.

It began innocently enough. John Rittenhouse broke the chattering by raising his voice and saying, "I'm going to take a risk. Eve and I almost didn't come tonight. I don't want to be bored. Maybe it's one of my hangups, but I can't stand to be bored."

Eve agreed. They had sat in their car for a minute before coming in, wondering if they really wanted to be there.

Margaret Kenan said she had been thinking all week about something from Plato she had heard: "There is no evil that can touch the good man." Several persons reacted quizzically. They weren't sure they believed that. What did it mean?

Anne said the words were actually Socrates' at the time of his trial and execution, and that the same thing was exemplified in the death of Jesus. I agreed, and recalled some Scottish preacher's having depicted the agonizing death of Jesus on the cross and then saying to his congregation, "Behold, the safest man in the world."

We talked for a while about how freedom and vulnerability are really inseparable—that no man is truly free until he is completely open and accessible to others. Some seemed to understand and some dldn't. John did. He spoke of the amazing change that had come over his life in the last two years. He had moved from a performance orientation to an acceptance orientation, and no longer felt compelled to succeed at anything. He could actually perform better, he said, because now he was free not to. Life had become a joy.

"Sometimes I can't believe it," he said, "life is so rich. Like the last couple of days. I have felt so great that I even believe in heaven again. Not because of anything anybody says, or any proof, but just because I want to. I was on a plane, and I thought, 'If anything happens and the plane goes down, I'm going to fight to crawl out of that wreckage and walk away because I want to live. But if I don't live, that's not the end. What I've found just won't die.'" One or two others agreed; they knew.

Eve testified that John had been much easier to live with since the change.

The talk about performance and acceptance lured Ellen Harris into the conversation. "I want to ask you all something," she said. "I want to know how you feel about me. Am I only a necessary evil to you? I get this feeling that I am."

There was obvious passion in Ellen's voice. No one else spoke for a few moments. There was an electric feeling in the room, as if we had all been charged by something and were waiting for the lightning to discharge it.

The lightning came from Eve's side of the room.

"Ellen," she said, "I believe you mean that question, and I admire your courage for asking it. Yes, I think you **are** a necessary evil."

Eve went on to explain what she meant. Ellen had been in

charge of a circle to which she belonged, and had been rather arbitrary in making program assignments. She had also taken charge when Helen Roos's husband had died, several months earlier, and had solicited persons to take food in and to plan a birthday party for Helen's son. Something about the way she had done these things had irritated Eve. Organization was important; Eve knew and admitted that. But she resented the way Ellen always seemed to impose it on people.

Rachel Anstruther agreed. She had not liked Ellen's tendency to want to organize others. She knew it needed to be done, but something about the way Ellen did it brought out the worst in her.

The discussion of reactions to Ellen went on for half an hour. Most of those who took part in it affirmed Ellen as a good and likeable person, yet admitted that she had rubbed them the wrong way on a number of occasions. I looked at her husband Vernon several times and noted that he was intensely perturbed. At first he had responded openly with a joke: "I've known for several years that she is a necessary evil." But his lip began to quiver, and once I thought he seemed to be talking to himself very rapidly, almost frenziedly.

It was Anne who exhibited the most concern for Ellen, I thought. "Ellen," she said when we finally came to a lull, "how do you feel?"

Ellen had a hard time forming the words. She could barely speak. When she did talk, her words were almost inaudible, but they were obviously heartfelt. "I feel . . . that you all care about me," she said.

I think Ellen really meant this. Sometimes we think it is heartless to tell people how we really feel about them. But this often results in their feeling, even at a subconscious level, that they are not in touch with us. They know there is a hidden barrier between us, a shield that prevents communication. It may be more Christlike to speak honestly and openly to people about our true feelings than it is to be polite and uncommitted to them in any way. As Judy Quillian said, "This is a **different** group. Most places, you wouldn't say anything hostile to anybody else. You would just coexist without clearing the air between you." Ellen actually discerned the care of the group through the agony of confrontation. And, afterwards, those who confronted her were able to affirm her, whereas before they had resented her too much to offer her affirmation.

Somehow the focus of conversation had shifted momentarily to Rachel Anstruther. She was talking about how she tended to intellectualize things, and to enjoy the analytical process, instead of allowing herself to experience them emotionally. Eve, who was turned on as the catalyst of the evening, countered her by saying that, on the contrary, she thought Rachel was welling with emotion but simply managed to stifle it most of the time. Rachel admitted this was true. She was feeling very emotional at the moment. It was just that in our society we learn not to share our emotions with persons outside the home.

I recalled that one of my students had recently written a sermon about crying. People ought to cry in front of each other, he said, as an act of sharing. Without explanations or anything. Just cry when they feel like it.

Rachel began to shed big tears. She shook her head and wiped her eyes and said, "I don't know why I'm doing this. I'm not unhappy. I'm just doing it."

We felt very close to one another.

Dan Quillian had come in late sometime during the evening, and had been sitting quietly, listening and observing. Judy had told us he was involved in a zoning case in a council meeting a few miles out of town, and would probably come by if he arrived home in time. At this point Eve turned to him and noted that it was unnatural for him to be so quiet. She wanted to hear from him.

Dan said he was sorry to have missed whatever he missed, because he could tell something had been going on. Ellen looked different, he said. He didn't know why, or what had happened, but she just affected him as a different person from the Ellen he had known. As for being quiet, he was just enjoying himself. And, quite frankly, he had a reentry problem. He had spent the day in the courtroom and the evening in a council room dealing with lawyers and people who were "trained to be dishonest" with one another. He had played the game as well as the next. He liked his work. He enjoyed the game. But it took him a while to readjust when he left it. What was going on in this room was of a totally different nature.

Eve went after him. She wanted to know who the real Dan Quillian was. She thought he was **always** playing games—with us as well as with the people in court.

Rachel Anstruther agreed; she and Bob had often wondered who Dan was. They had gone so far as to phone Judy once and tell her they would like to know.

It seemed to me that Dan was suddenly in his element again. For a person who likes the center of the floor, it was an enviable position. How did he know who he was? he asked. He was good at playing roles; he loved it; he could always play roles, even in grammar school.

"It isn't how much you know in life," he said; "I learned that early. It's how well you can fool people. And I've always been successful at it. I can't believe how good I am. I really am. I like what I do. I'd rather be in the courtroom than anywhere else on earth. I have never failed. Why should I want to know who I am, or be any different? I'm happy the way things are. Dan Quillian is a success."

Judy shot out at him, "That was a horse's ass thing to say!"

"You've admitted to one failure," said Eve.

"What's that?"

"You don't know who you are."

Several times Dan tried to let the matter drop, but Eve was insistent. Finally he reacted vituperatively: he was not going to be goaded into spilling his guts. He knew Eve was trained in encounter techniques, and he didn't "give a damn for all that sensitivity crap." Why couldn't people relate to each other on an upper-level basis instead of a lower-level basis? What was wrong with laughing and joking and playing roles with each other? Wasn't that a bonafide way of getting together? Why was it necessary to bare one's soul? How did we know what the soul was anyway? What did Eve want of him? What should he do?

"Bleed," said Anne.

But Dan wasn't going to bleed. He said he wasn't.

I was puzzled by two things. First, why had Eve pulled Dan's string? He had been sitting quietly, listening, when she had called him out to do his act, to perform for the group. What compulsion led to her attack on him? What did she really want from him? Second, was Dan really serious about not caring about who he was? If he was, what would happen to him when he finally encountered true failure? I voiced this concern to him, and told him about the conversation we had had earlier, the one about performance and acceptance.

"We talked about how freedom and vulnerability, freedom and accessibility, go hand in hand," I said. "Is it possible that you are hooked to a success-performance syndrome? What would happen if your act caved in, if you just stopped playing the game? Does the secret fear of that keep you going?"

For the first time, I thought, he seemed to be listening. He recognized something.

"Dan," said Eve, "you're great at summations. Really

great. You can always step in and add it up for the rest of us. But you don't really interact during the process. You don't share yourself. You keep that back."

Again Dan bristled with resistance. It wasn't going any further, he declared; he would not let it.

"I'm exhausted," said Eve; "you've really worn me out. And I'm frustrated, because you've held out on us. We could have had something together, but you wouldn't. That frustrates me."

"I like this group," said Dan. "I don't have to get anything out of it. I don't expect anything from it. I just like to be in it. I just like to come and be here."

"I'm not through with you," said Eve.

Everybody stood. Several persons stretched. It had been a long, hard session.

Eve crossed the room immediately and kissed Dan. I went over and put my arm around Judy and put my hand on Dan's head and pushed on it a couple of times. Outside, I heard afterwards, Eve and Ellen embraced and Eve said, "You're quite a woman after all, aren't you?" Feelings were high all around.

Dan and Judy lingered until everyone else had left. The group was meeting at our place for the month. We sank back into the easiest chairs in the room.

"I wasn't going to let her get me," Dan said. "I would have lied before I would have let her get me."

We talked about success and failure. Dan and I felt a sense of camaraderie born of mutual professional respect. He expressed this to me. I talked about my own "golden touch," and what I thought it had done to me. I had hit the "emptiness plateau" half a dozen years ago, when I was about the age of Dan now. What I said was that it wasn't so bad. I felt a lot better now, a lot securer, than I had. My experience had been essentially the same as John's: I no longer had to perform. And it was great. The acceptance of failure was great. Once you managed that, no evil could really touch you. What was obvious was that Dan did have tremendous reserves of human care and tenderness. And it was also obvious why Judy had appeared to be on Eve's side in going after him: she knew his real qualities, and wanted more than anything for him to show them to the group.

It was after midnight when Dan and Judy left. Anne and I talked as we got ready for bed. It had been a fascinating evening, but for some undefinable reason we were slightly depressed. What was it that was nagging us? Maybe it was the fragility of human beings, and the consequent fragility of human relationships. People had admitted to Ellen that they had discussed their resentments of her behind her back. Why are people this way?

And the predominance of Eve's role in the evening bothered us. Somehow—by her very preoccupation with honesty perhaps—she had brought us into sight of the demonic. We had felt it, smelled it, tasted it. It was there in the room with us. The depths of evil had opened for a little while, just as surely as they do in the world of Hawthorne's novels, and we had witnessed it.

We had recently seen a television drama about New England witches. Eve's association with what had happened, her catalytic act in the encounter, necessitated our linking her, however tentatively and imaginatively, with witchcraft. We did not mean it derogatorily. What had happened was good; it would work out for good with all of us. But our closeness to the workings of good and evil nevertheless prompted the mental association.

So many important things came out in this meeting that it would be impossible to elaborate on all of them. Four items in particular must be noticed:

(1) John's decision to take a risk was a significant event for all of us. It was definitely a risk. He had no way of knowing how what he said would be received. Someone might have said to him, "John, if you are so afraid of being bored, why don't you go on to a movie?" But the risk he took drew Ellen out to take a risk of her own, and then Eve was willing to take a risk too. The whole evening turned on that initial decision of John's to gamble on the reaction of the group to his honesty.

There is far too little risk-taking in our relationships with each other. What this probably means is that we are very unsure of the relationships. We don't know whether they will bear the strain of different opinions and feelings. We play it safe and conservative, harboring secret reactions and emotions lest they prove unacceptable to others. Eventually we don't know any more whether we can really entrust our true feelings to other people. Even husbands and wives guard against revealing their inner selves to each other.

If the Christian faith is about any one thing, it is about forgiveness and acceptance. It is about a man who died while forgiving his torturers, and about the Divine Spirit who forgives even those who frustrate this attempt to bring all beings into unity with himself. One of its favorite stories is the parable of the son who left home and spent his father's money, then was welcomed back with joyous emotion, and of an elder son who was chided by the father for being peevish and resentful over the lavish reception his brother received.

We need to practice more risk-taking in the context of Christian fellowship, and establish new habits of honesty and candor in interpersonal relationships. Risk ought to become a daily matter among us. Otherwise forgiveness and acceptance can never seem very real to us. Without venturing anything of our real selves and real attitudes, we never know how others feel about our feelings and opinions. We have a private sense of guilt about the thoughts we keep to ourselves, and seldom realize the joy of being accepted for who we are and how we feel.

(2) John put his finger on another weak spot—or is it really the same one?—when he spoke of his performance need which he felt he had overcome.

Most of us never fully overcome this need. We never feel sure enough of ourselves, confident enough of how we will be accepted, merely to be who we know we are. We have to play a role for other people, and build ourselves into people we are not—into heroes, intellects, sophisticates, athletes, perfect mates, and so on.

The truth is—and it is much easier to recognize than to internalize—people don't really like us for being perfect, they like us for being imperfect.

We put on the show for them because we think they won't like us as we really are. We don't like ourselves as we really are, and we don't think anyone else will either.

But think about the people you really like, really adore. Is it because of their strong points or their weak points? Nine times out of ten, it is their weaknesses that attract us to them. For example, think of someone you know who is always making darn fool statements and then trying to get out of them. His tendency to get himself in over his head is an idiosyncrasy that attracts you to him. You smile when you think about him. His shortcoming makes him more human to you. You feel much easier in his presence than you do in the presence of someone who is invariably right. You can take more risks yourself when you are with him.

We spend so much psychical energy trying to keep our masks on straight when we are in a group or with someone we are unsure of—so much, in fact, that we don't have much left for being our real selves, for laughing, feeling, and enjoying our selves. Some people just freeze inside when they get in a group. Everything about them becomes stiff and awkward. Nothing they say comes out right. They worry about their posture, their hands, their faces, their hair-dos—everything. Their breathing becomes shallow and tight. They feel unnatural and abnormal, and think everyone else is noticing. The truth is they **are** unnatural. This is not the way they really are. They are performing instead of being themselves.

People relate to us much more easily on the basis of our weaknesses than on the basis of our strengths. We shouldn't be afraid to reveal our weaknesses. It may seem a terrible risk to lay them out in front of others for a change. But it is amazing how quickly other people relate to us this way, and how comfortable we are with them in this new situation.

(3) Relationships are often strengthened by confrontation. Here again our instincts are usually wrong. We suppose that confrontation is what destroys relationships, so we try to shield them from friction.

What if Eve had not been so bold in answering Ellen when Ellen said she felt hidden resentment in the reactions of others toward her? Suppose we had all merely denied Ellen's suspicions, and said, "Oh no, Ellen, you're mistaken, surely no one could resent you." In that case Ellen would have felt momentary reassurance but would have soon begun to sense something in the air between her and other people again. She would have known something was wrong but wouldn't have been any closer to putting her finger on it than she was before.

The confrontation was painful. There is no point in denying that. Confrontations always are. But then so are injections at the doctor's office. The point is, they clear the air and make it possible for honest healing to occur. Ellen's suspicions were confirmed, and her friends were able to talk to her specifically about what they resented in her manner. And, when it was over, she not only knew more precisely how to interact with people in the future, but felt the firm friendship and support of others beneath the level of resentment and bad feelings. She received the kind of assurance which we try to impart to children when we disapprove of things they have done, that she was loved and affirmed despite the particular actions which others had regarded as negative or unpleasant. Her summation, "I feel that you care," was an extremely important lesson to all of us. Our acceptance by others is not totally dependent on whether they like or dislike our attitudes and behavior.

Eve and others expressed virtually the same kind of care to Dan, who showed reluctance to deal with the climate of unreality about his projected personality in the group. He was not prepared, on that particular evening, to expose his inner self completely, and so continued to fence with Eve and Rachel in a kind of verbal duel. They were saying essentially the same thing to him that had been said to Ellen, namely, "Dan, you are putting us on a lot, and we don't like this in you." But he was not ready, as Ellen had been, to admit that he sensed this and regretted it. Yet they were saying also, by bothering to confront him at all and then by staying with the matter until he became annoyed, "Dan, we really care about you, and that is why we want you to level with us and let us in on your hidden self."

Many people complain that one of the main problems with the church today is that people in the local fellowships seem so unreal. Existence in the church is shadowy and ethereal, as though substanceless ghosts were meeting and passing right through one another without noticing.

One reason for this is doubtless the habit we get into of wanting to be pleasant, especially in the church. Some people have the attitude that the church is the last place in the world where there should be disagreements or unpleasantness. They may argue and confront other people regularly at home, at school, at work, in the supermarket, or in other places, but they bite their tongues and tiptoe by one another in church, smiling and shaking hands and behaving as politely as they know how. And the ministers only confirm this tendency by trying to keep all controversial thoughts, words, and actions out of the worship and out of the sermon. But we cannot really love without engaging in honest confrontation. The clash and contact are themselves vital to human relationships. They discharge the static electricity which builds up between persons and groups and which is far less harmful when discharged than when stored up and refused release.

Most of us, if we are honest with ourselves, will admit that the persons we recall most affectionately and clearly from our childhoods are persons we stood in some tension with. For some reason, we feel bound to them by invisible cords which do not link us to other persons. It is a kind of kinship born of battle, a relationship that has grown out of a personal struggle which others were not involved in. The thing is, they are **real** to us in a way people we didn't engage with aren't.

We need to cultivate more the sense of caring, honest confrontation with those whose ways of expression or interaction give us difficulty. Most of the time we will find that the psychologists are right in saying that dislike or even hate is more closely related to love than indifference is, and that we will discover how much we genuinely care about those whom we engage in open confrontation.

(4) Experiences of closeness through conflict and love often result in physical contact between those most intimately involved. Words did not seem adequate to express the warmth of relationships which we felt that

night. People naturally embraced, kissed, and patted each other.

Perhaps we ought not to judge too quickly the secular encounter groups in which physical contact is stressed almost at the outset. Our culture has imposed a lot of hangups about the body on us. If it hadn't, all the exploitation of body which is so visible in novels, movies, advertising, and commercialized sex would not be possible. We relate very little to the world around us through the medium of our bodies, and the very repression of our attitudes makes us easy prey to certain kinds of sexual fantasies and perversions.

The famous Gestalt psychologist Fritz Perls says that one of the major problems most of us have is that we set boundaries to our selves that are too limited. Boundaries, he thinks, are the number one cause of friction between people and nations; disputes and wars always begin as border clashes; if there were no clear borders, there would be fewer conflicts. We assume that our skin is a boundary between us and other persons, forgetting that no organism is complete in itself but depends on a much larger environment for its survival. Therefore we hesitate to touch others or be touched by them unless we are already on very intimate terms with them. We consider touching to be a border violation.

Is it possible that people in the church have been too much concerned about such violations? Does such concern really square with what we say about the way Christ's death has made us one in love and compassion for one another? We sanction physical contact in moments of unusual stress or release, associated with disaster or religious fervor; for example, embracing is proper at the time of a death or a marriage or a baptism. Why do we frown upon it as a normal, everyday mode of relationship?

This is a matter which we all need to explore more

openly in discussion and even in practice. When Eve kissed Dan and later hugged Ellen, she was saying to them nonverbally more strongly than she could ever have said with mere words, "I really care for you; I am obliterating the false boundaries which have been set up between us." To be sure, physical touch is subject to all kinds of unloving exploitations. But that is hardly a reason for rejecting its potentialities for good in our lives.

7

Reactions have been crackling all week. Ellen called us early the following morning and talked to each of us for half an hour. She and Vernon had slept very little. She was hurt that people had been unable to confront her individually with their resentments, and had conferred outside of her presence about her. She wondered if Eve derived pleasure from probing the weaknesses of others. Ellen had not realized what a can of worms she had really been opening when she asked for people's opinions about her. But she was okay. She would come out on top.

We were out of town for the weekend. On Monday Ellen and Vernon dropped by and had tea with Anne, as they were both on vacation. Vernon was upset about Eve's manner of attacking people. He and Ellen both mentioned that it had bothered them to watch John massaging Helen Roos's shoulders as she sat on the floor in front of his chair at one point in the evening.

On Tuesday Anne attended a Women of the Church meeting, and had lunch with Margaret Kenan, Rachel Anstruther, Marnie Jones, and Barney Hopkins. Barney had apparently been besieged by calls from a number of persons in the group, focusing primarily on three things: concern for Ellen and Dan, who, they seemed to feel in retrospect, were severely dealt with; discomfort for Eve's obsessive need for confrontation as a basis for relationship; and uneasiness about the way John "caressed" Helen's shoulders. Barney had apparently even talked to Helen, and she assured him that it had not bothered her.

"Hell," said Marnie, "she needed it."

Margaret and Rachel both defended Eve.

Barney was worried about the group; he would participate more fully in it himself, he said, if there were a trained leader present. As it was, he was fearful that we would do irreparable damage to each other. The others assured him that they thought the group cared too much for that; it supported as much as it tested and tore away.

I confess that I have a very uneasy feeling about the whole thing. It bothers me to see what has happened in the wake of the meeting. Several persons who were swept along with the group in confronting Ellen and Vernon have evidently had second thoughts. They seem to be afraid their turn will come too. And now they are consolidating against Eve and John as a divisive couple. I may be wrong. Maybe they aren't, really. But it worries me that I think they are, because I see this as the pattern of groups everywhere, that the weak and frightened people unite in misunderstanding the free persons who threaten them. It's like what happened in Ibsen's **Enemy of the People**. And I don't want it to happen to Eve and John.

"I've got something to say," Ellen began last night. "But first I want Dick [Hofman] to lead us in prayer. I want us to pray that you will understand what I am going to say in a spirit of love, because that is how it is meant."

Oh-oh, I thought, this is it; Ellen has regrouped and is coming back for the attack. I wasn't ready to pray, because I felt that Ellen was unconsciously using prayer as a manipula-

tive device, and I didn't feel like being manipulated. I looked
at the floor, but I didn't close my eyes. I had the feeling that
others were staring open-eyed too.

Dick's prayer was primarily a thanksgiving for community,
and the sense that people care. I thought as he prayed, he has
a wonderful sense of what it's all about—he cares about
people.

When he finished, Ellen began. It didn't come out at all
as I had expected it to. She had had a lot of reaction to what
happened last week, she said. She was terribly hurt by some
of the things that were said, and especially by the fact that
people had not told her these things privately before, even
though they confessed to having felt them a long time. She
was also concerned about the group's procedures. What if
the thing she had gone through had happened to someone
less stable than she? Couldn't it have destroyed the person?
She guessed she was talking about putting some kind of limit
on what goes on in the group, and that the limit, instead of
being some artificial measuring stick, should be love. Nothing
should be said that is not said in love.

Her husband Vernon was worried too. As an estate counselor for a local banking institution, he dealt frequently with
people in disturbed and critical periods of their lives. He had
learned how to talk to them, had developed ways of dealing
with them. But even then, he said, his methods simply didn't
work with some people. And he was afraid of the volatility of
this group—we simply did not know enough about what was
going on in people's minds.

Someone asked Ellen if she didn't feel that she had been
dealt with in love. She had said that what happened to her
was "beautiful," and that it had had its positive side as well
as its negative side. Couldn't she wish for others to have the
same beautiful experience?

At some point in the discussion, Adele Hofman said that

she had been made very uncomfortable by what happened at the last meeting. She wanted the group to relate on a different plane, and to talk about good experiences, not bad ones.

Eve Rittenhouse had been silent through the preceding conversations. Now she admitted that she felt uncomfortable because she believed that she was implied in what Adele had just said and in many of the other things that had been verbalized. She would like for Adele to talk about what kind of group she really wanted this to be.

Adele was reluctant. Eve persisted. She truly wanted to hear Adele talk, to hear her say what informed her desires for the kind of group it should be and what kind of group it would be if it met those desires.

"I don't want to talk about it," said Adele, "but I guess if I have the opportunity I shouldn't pass it up." She sat quietly for a minute, thinking where to begin.

She talked about being raised in a nominally religious home, and characterized her religious experience as "lukewarm." It was an upper-middle-class home, and she received all the material benefits her parents could provide, including private schooling, college, and summer camps. She married Dick and they moved to Texas, where he was an office man for an oil company. They were active in the church, but weren't satisfied with the quality of their religious experience. Dick was restless. He thought maybe he was being called to the ministry. That was all right; it would mean going to Austin to seminary, and she could envision life in Austin. But then he thought maybe it was a call to mission work in the Congo. That was out! She wasn't ready to go that far. Her furniture was a symbol of her rootedness to the status quo: she and Dick slept in a bed that had been in her family for 160 years, and she was not about to leave that behind to go to the Congo!

Then something happened that had changed her life. She was working as a counselor at a summer church camp, somewhere in the mountains. Word came to her in the wilderness that she had a telegram from home. A minister friend, Jack, had driven her to the nearest telephone to call the Western Union office. When they arrived at the telephone, they couldn't get anything but a busy signal from Western Union. (Later they discovered that someone had left the phone off the cradle for half an hour at the office.) All sorts of tragic possibilities crossed her mind as she waited. When she finally did get through, the message concerned a pet dog which had been lost at the time she left for camp.

"Chico is found stop hooray stop hooray," read the message.

"But Jack didn't think I was silly for the things I imagined while we were waiting," she said. "I felt I could trust him and talk to him about how I was feeling." So one night after their counselor duties were over, she and Jack sat in the front of a truck and talked until 3 in the morning. Apparently she spilled out her loneliness and confusion to him. He told her that he had felt that way too—until one day when he had a second religious experience that changed his life.

That night Adele had had a second religious experience too. "I don't know how to describe it," she said, "except to say that everything has been different since then. I have been a different person. Before that, the world was black-and-white; now everything is in technicolor."

Afterwards, she had been willing to go to the Congo or anywhere else God wanted them to go. They had talked to a church official about going, but had decided that that was not what God was seeking them for. There were too many factors against it. They had difficulty with languages and they would probably have to send their daughter to boarding school if they went. But they did feel led to come to work for

the church's board in this city, and took a big cut in salary
to follow that leading.

Adele must have talked uninterrupted for at least thirty
minutes. Her voice was quiet and pleasant, and everyone
listened attentively.

But when she was through, Eve said, "Adele, I still want
to hear you talk about what you expect from the group. I
have the feeling that you have a hidden design you would
like to impose on the group, or that you want the group to
assume, and I want to hear from you what it is."

"I just want the group to talk about God," she said. "Everybody seems embarrassed to use the word 'God' or to talk
about what he has done in their lives."

Dot Hopkins said she thought the word "embarrassed"
was the key, that most of us shy away from talking about God
because we have overreacted against an overtly religious culture and are sensitive about using God-talk.

I said I didn't think Dot should include us all in her analysis, that some of us were not embarrassed to talk about God,
but were perhaps embarrassed at the poverty of our language
for talking about him. I spoke directly to Adele. "It's funny,"
I said, "but God becomes more and more anonymous to me.
The more I think I know him the more impossible it becomes
for me to say where he is or how he is acting."

"But God is so important to me," said Adele. "I have to
talk about him. He is more important to me than my husband
or my children. It wouldn't be natural not to talk about him."

"I don't feel that way," I said. "I once did, but I don't anymore. People are more important to me now than God. I find
him in people. I love them and I feel very comfortable about
him."

Rachel Anstruther said it more beautifully: "Adele, we do
love God. I love him. But I love him in the soil, in the earth,

in the world around me." She said much more, but these are words I remember. I had tears in my eyes from the beauty of it when she finished. Bob Anstruther was sitting on the floor. "Gosh, Adele," he said, "I feel God too. I feel the Holy Spirit. But I don't always feel the need to verbalize it. Like last week. When that business was going on with Ellen, I felt that the Holy Spirit was here. I really did. But I didn't say it like that. We were in the midst of a conversation, and I didn't think it mattered that I felt that. If I had said it, it might have interrupted what we were doing."

"May I say something?" asked Liz. "You all know I don't talk much. Ellen said to me this week, 'Liz, you were awfully quiet last week,' and I was, and the week before that, and the week before that too. I opened up and told you my story one night because I had to, but I've kept quiet a lot since then because I've never been sure whether what I had to say was relevant or irrelevant.

"I sit here in agony sometimes wondering whether to talk or not, and I know there are others in this room who feel the same way, and that's the reason we don't hear from them. I talk about God, and I praise him for saving me from alcoholism. And I go to church now and I'm not just an eleven-till-twelve Christian. But I'm like John says, I meet God in all the people around me. I feel him in this group when we talk about our problems and hangups. I feel him in AA when we talk about our drinking problem there."

Anne, who remembered with anguish the night she had opened the God-talk matter, bore in on Barney Hopkins about why he didn't "jump all over" Liz the way she thought he had attacked her that night. She felt that Barney was making a spiritual judgment and was unfairly labeling the Hofmans as Christian and her as sub-Christian.

At first Barney said it was because she reminded him of his own difficulty right now of distinguishing between Christianity and humanism, and he felt that humanism, while it was fine in its way, didn't go far enough. He obviously felt that we ought to talk about God and the Spirit in very conscious ways in our meetings.

Anne persisted. Why didn't he attack Liz too?

Finally Barney admitted it was because he thought Liz was weak and Anne was strong.

"But I'm not, Barney," she said. "I'm not."

Liz said she knew it. "That girl's sent up signal after signal," she said, "and nobody ever picks them up. Last week she left the room to put Eric to bed and she was crying when she came back and she said 'Do you ever just feel unloved?' We took it she was talking about Eric, but she was talking about her. **She** felt unloved, and not a darned one of us picked it up and talked to her about it!"

"I know," said Rachel. "Bob and I talked about that after we went home. We remembered that she had come back in and said that, and we realized that no one had responded. We just left her dangling."

"If you don't have esteem for yourself," said Anne, "I guess no one else can."

Dan Quillian spoke up. "I think I ought to tell you how I've felt. Not now, not since last week, but up till then. I felt real negative about you and John. Not negative negative—not like that. But positive negative. I mean, I thought you were more than human. You just sorta seemed to be on this cloud up above everybody else."

"Oh, no, Anne," said Rachel, "I liked you the minute I met you."

"Well, that's how I felt," said Dan.

"I can appreciate that," said Anne. "I really can."

Barney and Anne talked some more. She accused him of

not listening to her, of having a mental image of what she was like and then failing to see her as a person. Once, she seemed to feel at a loss to go further. "Can I say something?" I said. "I'm going to speak as a husband watching from the sidelines. I don't think any of you knew how agonizingly alone we felt when we got into this group. When either of us ventured to say anything, we felt as if our voices were trembling. We didn't know if we were making any contact. That was the way Anne felt that night when she made the speech about God-talk. She overstated her case—**way** overstated it, in my opinion. But she had been planning that speech for a week, planning her effort to get in touch with you. If what she said was distorted, it was because of all the pressure that had built up behind what she said, behind the mere words. I know why she said what she did, and I think I know why you heard what you heard. She just wanted to make contact."

By now it was obvious that she was making contact. She and Eve were holding hands. She felt spent, but I think she knew she was in.

It was Eve who spoke next. She didn't know whether she could come back to the group again. Someone had called her and told her that there was a lot of talk going around about what had happened last Thursday night. "I can handle what happens here," she said, "but I don't have time to keep up with twenty-five people and what goes on in private conversations all week. I need some assurance that what we say here is held in confidence. I'm not going to talk about you during the week, and I want the same courtesy from you."

Rachel agreed. She understood that even some people who were not in the group had been talking about some of the things that had been said.

The Hofmans and Joneses had already left to relieve their babysitters. Now it was nearly midnight, and the others were tired and needed to leave. Saying goodnight was an act of love. I went to the front door to hand out coats and bid our friends Godspeed. Eve and I put our arms around each other as she went out. "Don't drop out on us, Eve," I said. "Please." "You're something else," she said.

Mindy Carson and I stood talking for a moment, and I bent over and kissed her forehead. When Barney came by, he and I hugged each other tightly and held on for a moment. "Tell Anne 'thank you' before you go to bed tonight. She helped me," he said.

Afterwards Anne said they had both hugged and cried, and Vernon Harris had hugged her too. We were all worn out and happy.

Eve's point was well taken. Nothing is more destructive to group confidence than extracurricular discussion of what has taken place, particularly with persons who are not members of the group. Factionalism almost inevitably develops within the group when this occurs, and conversations and reactions are often distorted. It is important in any sharing group that absolute confidence be "written in" as one of the group's ground rules at all times. The relationships established within the group are as sacred and personal as the relationship between minister and counselee, doctor and patient, or lawyer and client. This fact is so vital that it ought to be reiterated from time to time, lest members of the group forget and betray the trust of others.

The phone began ringing early yesterday morning. Liz called and wanted Anne to go with her to Cheekwood for lunch Saturday and then to see the Christmas trees. Dot Hopkins called and asked her to go to lunch at Cross-Keys Restaurant at 12:30, and Judy Quillian called and asked her to come over for coffee in mid-morning. Before she was ready to leave for Judy's the doorbell rang and there were Ellen and Vernon Harris. We sat and chatted for half an hour, and then they drove ahead of Anne to show her the way to Judy's which she had forgotten since the night we had our first group meeting at her house.

"How do you feel this morning?" asked Ellen.

"Sort of empty," said Anne.

She didn't mean that she didn't feel good. She was tired, and, as she confessed to me that night, she just sort of wanted to hug herself and not talk about what had happened. She wanted to savor it all by herself.

Vernon said he thought the group was doing miraculous things for all of us. "We have been half-sick from loneliness the last five years," he said. "I come home from work some nights and can't wait to get back to people who care about me and love me. Work is so impersonal."

"I know what you mean," I said. I had felt that way too.

It was a funny thing, though, that after they left and I went to the university and had lunch with some professors, I felt that I gave the professors a better chance and had a more enjoyable time with them than usual. I asked what they were doing in their courses, and we talked about some experiences with modern art, which seemed to stem from something one of them had been talking about in his course. Maybe my desert is beginning to bloom.

When I came in at dinnertime, Anne said she had had a wonderful day. She and Judy had talked for an hour and a half, and she had stayed with the Quillians' smallest child while Judy took another child to nursery school. At lunch, she and Dot had talked very intimately about what had happened the night before. Dot said she and Barney had stayed up practically all night talking. He had felt exhilarated.

Anne said she knew Dot had resented the way she attacked Barney.

"How did you know that?" asked Dot.

"Any woman would," said Anne; "I wouldn't think much of you if you had not."

When they parted, she said, Dot grasped her hand and said, "I'm so glad we've found each other. Our friendship can grow and grow."

"But we won't force it," said Anne. "We'll **let** it grow."

8

Our group has not met over the holidays. It has been almost four weeks since we had a real session. On the Thursday night before Christmas we had a party and exchanged silly gifts. Dick and Adele Hofman brought a boxful of clever items for "the person in an encounter group"—headache tablets, barf bags, etc.

This had a particular significance because Adele had had a bad week. She had left the meeting the week before feeling terribly rejected. We had dinner with her and Dick on Saturday night and spent four or five hours talking about her sense of isolation. She had told her whole story the other night, and it hadn't made a damned bit of difference to anybody.

"What did you want us to do?" we asked.

"I don't know," she said, "but I felt that nobody cared."

We suspected she was pouting because she had not been able to maneuver the group, to get it to adopt her particular religious perspective. The group had essentially said to her that its religious experience was higher than hers, even though she considered hers to be a kind of mountaintop thing.

Sunday morning we sat immediately behind the Hofmans in church. Barney preached an Advent sermon which, as well as I can recall it now, spoke of the Incarnation as something which demanded that we consider the presence of God in secular existence, especially in other persons. Adele was agitated, and bolted out as soon as the service was over. That night she did not attend the family-night supper and carol party. Dick said she was feeling awful and he didn't know what to do when she was in a mood like that.

On Monday, she called Anne and said she felt much better. We hoped it was so, and that she was not "coming around" because no one was making a special effort to reach her in her self-imposed isolation. At any rate, she and Dick showed up at the party.

There was a lot of silliness and fun the night of the party. But several persons remarked that they felt "cheated" and "let down" because we were not continuing the intense kind of searching and relationship that had characterized the previous Thursday night. It seemed strange, hearing that: people preferring something else to a party.

Anne and I frankly enjoyed the respite from the group during the holidays. We saw several of the persons at church and at parties and dinners, but always in the company of other people. The fall had been extremely strenuous, and we were tired.

We were so tired, in fact, that we let some old friends down. Two nights before Christmas we had just come in from celebrating Hanukkah with Jewish friends. The phone rang. Old friends in another state were on the line. They wanted to come to see us on Christmas day and spend a week with us. We invited them to come on, but afterwards, as we sat down, we realized how utterly exhausted we were and what this would mean in terms of the rest we had expected to get over Christmas. We slept very little that night. What could we do?

The next morning, I telephoned the friends and said,

"Look, we are so thoroughly depleted just now that we would be very poor company. Can you delay the visit two or three days and give us a chance to catch our breath?"

They were pleasant enough about it, but decided that day to change their plans entirely. They phoned from a motel in Pittsburgh, saying they were going to their parents' home in the West. I urged them to come back by our place on their return and they said they might. Up to now we have not seen them or heard from them.

We have felt bad about this, but not guilty. The experience with the group has enabled us to speak more frankly to friends, even at the risk of losing them. In the long run, we are convinced, our relationships will be healthier because of it.

We meet again tonight. There is a kind of electric feeling among those we have seen. What will happen? How will people relate after an interval of nearly a month? Will we have lost something? Or, like a good night's sleep in a person's life, will the break have been good for the group?

The meeting was a bust, probably by common consent. Nothing happened. We met at the Quillians' house. Everyone seemed glad to see everyone else, and there was a lot of small talk. But nothing big ever got going.

Ellen Harris tried once to get us to talk about "what God had done in our lives," proceeding around the room from person to person.

The first person who spoke up, Judy Quillian, pretty well demolished the idea. "How do you know what God is doing?" she asked, her eyes burning with spritely passion. She described a recent event in her life. Her brother had gotten married to an apparently stunning young woman who said she did not believe in God. The couple had wanted to marry without a clergyman, but had submitted to his parents' desire and had called up a Presbyterian minister whom none of the family knew. They were all very conscious of the number of times he used the word "God" in the service and prayers. "Twenty-seven times," said Dan; "I counted."

"I spent one afternoon alone with the girl," said Judy, "and we talked about what we did and didn't believe. I tried to tell her how I believed in God. But, once you've said that much, what else is there to say? We got along real well, and had a great time, and I think she's tremendous, but I sure didn't witness very well to her."

"What did you expect to accomplish with her?" asked someone. "If you could have done what you wanted to do, what goals did you have in mind?"

Judy shook her head. She didn't know.

"Maybe you did witness to her," suggested Rachel Anstruther, "in the best way possible."

That was as far as it went. Someone mentioned a recent television program featuring the Children of God, a conservative communal type of young people's organization that appears to be spreading throughout the country, especially in the South. That led to a discussion of radicalism, and radicalism, in turn, to styles in politics. Some in the group were prepared to admit that they sympathized with radical types in our society today and felt that they did not do enough to support their sympathy with actual commitment. Others appeared to be threatened by such talk, and took rather strong stands against "unpatriotic" and "un-American" tendencies at work in the country.

The meeting broke up earlier than usual. Some began to leave a little after nine, and most of us had said goodbye by ten or shortly after. Each knew that the others were disappointed.

The two highlights of the evening, for me, were Judy's ingenuous report of her attempt to talk to her new sister-in-law about God, and the chance to know Bill Duval a little better. Bill had spoken out pretty firmly on the conservative side in our discussion about radicalism. Strangely enough, even though we disagreed on most things, I think we both felt closer for having talked openly and honestly about our feelings.

Anne expressed a sense of anger as we drove home. She didn't want to "waste" evenings away from the children. But that seems to be the price one pays for occasional high moments—without the discipline of meeting week after week, sometimes without any apparent results, there would never be any high moments.

Dan Quillian threw the ball out at the last meeting. "I have a question for the two ministers here that I think others in the group will be interested in," he said. "I want to know what you're supposed to say to a minister after the service if you liked his sermon. I faced the dilemma again Sunday morning with John. [I had preached in Barney's absence.] Do you say you 'enjoyed' the sermon? Should you enjoy a sermon? What do you guys want to hear when you've done well?"

Barney was quicker on the uptake than I, as he usually is: "A quiet handclasp with a $20 bill will be just fine, Dan." Laughter all around.

"I knew one minister," I said, "who reported having a man in his congregation who always registered his reaction to the sermon in terms of a baseball game. He would say, 'That was a two-bagger today, preacher,' or, 'You really knocked it out of the park today, preacher.' Sometimes he would even say, 'Boy, you popped that one up,' or, 'Go home and get in the shower.' " It was really a pretty effective and colorful medium of expression.

Conversation seemed to gravitate momentarily toward the

sermon I had preached, which was primarily a plea for treating other people as persons all the time. As a professor of preaching, I was especially interested in the feedback, to know whether people were hearing what I thought I was saying. The people in this group, at least, had really heard me, and had zeroed in on the most important idea in the sermon, namely, that we actually make objects of ourselves when we think we are making objects of others.

One of the things I wondered if they would notice was that there was nothing explicitly "religious" about the sermon. I had used the text, " 'Whoever says to his brother, You fool! will be in danger of the fires of hell' " (Matt. 5:22), and finally explained in the sermon that one meaning of that could be that we become useless objects when we have treated others as objects, and might as well be thrown on the fire and burned. In the end of the sermon, I suggested that one reason Jesus' personhood survived his death and became so legendary in the centuries ahead was his apparently infinite care for other people. Nothing was said about salvation, redemption, or resurrection—at least not by those terms.

"Let me pose a question for your response," I said. "Did you feel that there was anything missing in the sermon? A feeling of transcendence, for example? Was it all too horizontal, too concerned for interpersonal relationships? Was God left out?"

Amazingly, to me, no one felt that this was true.

"This is very interesting," I said. "Maybe it reveals something about you. I think a lot of people who heard a sermon like that one would complain that it wasn't a sermon because they hadn't heard any of the traditional language of a sermon. But you didn't feel that way. Maybe you are discovering God every day in places where he doesn't have to be named and in activities he doesn't have to be given credit for."

Barney said he did not feel like preaching without mentioning God. He had not got to that place in his thinking yet.

Someone spoke up at this point and said he did not like the implication of what was being said. "We are always talking," he said, "as if it is a good thing to get beyond talking a certain way. You know, if I grow a little bit I will stop saying 'God,' 'Christ,' and 'Holy Spirit' so much."

That was on target, I thought. We probably did give that impression.

I remembered a great man in one of my first parishes, a farmer who had been a coal miner in West Virginia in pre-union days and who had received only a fourth-grade education. He tended to lop off the prefixes and suffixes of polysyllabic words. I'll never forget how he always thanked the Lord for the blessings he had "stoweded" down upon us, or for having "hoped" us in the past.

"I'm sorry," I said, "if we give that impression. And we probably do." I told them about Willie, and said, "I'm sure there isn't a more authentic Christian in the world than he, and he talked the most primitive kind of God-talk I guess I've ever heard."

A lot more was said, but this was the train of thought. I regretted that I had talked more than I should have. No, I didn't, not really. The passion wasn't there again, and there seemed to be no point in not talking. At least the evening had more cohesion than the one last week.

Anne had come prepared to be bored again, and had brought a quilt she had been stitching on for several years. She put it down three or four times to say something, then picked it up again and went on stitching. Dan Quillian told her afterwards that he "missed" her. I did too.

We were also missing the Rittenhouses, who had not been back since Christmas. Eve especially, who was a catalyst. Anne and I said on the way home that we must try to contact them and urge them to come back.

It was Wednesday before we finally made the effort to reach them. We had tried casually two or three times and been told that their phone was temporarily disconnected. On Wednesday, though, Anne called the place where Eve had worked, and, after going through several channels, discovered that she and John had separated and moved away. Judy Quillian called and got the same story. She and Anne spent hours on the phone rehearsing what they knew of the Rittenhouses, trying to put together a plausible story to explain the sudden departure.

Later in the day, Judy called back to say that Dan had a letter in the mail from John. She hadn't opened it, but had tried to reach Dan at the office to ask if she could, and had failed to get in touch.

Anne said, "Why don't you and Dan come on over for dinner tonight and we can talk then?"

They did, and the conversation turned on the Rittenhouses most of the evening. John was in Texas, training for a new job he had taken in Atlanta, and Eve was living temporarily with her sister in New Jersey. We tried to telephone Eve, but could not get a listing for her, and we did not know her sister's name.

I think the thing that really bothered us, aside from the pain we felt for the Rittenhouses, was the feeling that we had all let them down at a crucial time in their lives. They could have told some of us, it is true; we didn't know. Still, we had not been open enough or inviting enough for them to want to do that.

"How many others in the group are we failing the same way?" asked Anne.

We didn't know. We suspected that we might find out at the next meeting. Dan said he was going to read John's letter then.

In his letter, John apologized to Dan and the members of the group for leaving so abruptly without even telling anyone what was happening. "Frankly," he said, "we were so confused and broken up during the brief time we had that we didn't want to inflict our sorrow on you. It isn't that we didn't think you'd care. We knew you would. We wanted to spare you the anguish we were feeling.

"This was a sudden thing to both of us. Oh, we had had our problems for a long time, but I thought we had worked them out and were real happy. I was happy. But Eve isn't satisfied with the way things were. We've agreed to separate for a while to see how we really feel about each other. Maybe it will work out later. Meanwhile, . . . "*

There was silence in the group for several minutes after the letter was read. Then two or three persons began to talk about a movie they had seen. We were all aware of pain, but the only thing people could talk about was a movie. It was almost as if the subject of the Rittenhouses' separation couldn't be discussed. It was tacitly forbidden.

Finally Anne could stand it no longer, and she headed straight into the matter.

"What is it with us?" she asked. "We failed them. I know we did. How many times did Eve sit over in the corner dying of agony, and we didn't do anything for her?"

Penny Duval, sitting on the floor in front of the fireplace, said she didn't think we had failed Eve. She had, in fact, met her for lunch numerous times and just listened to her problems. Eve and John, she felt, had complicated existences,

*This is a paraphrase from memory.

and the group had not let them down. If anything, they had failed to communicate their needs to the group.

Dan, who was studying the letter again, commented: "Let's see. This is dated the 18th. That means . . . John says he himself thought they were quite happy and contented until this thing happened. So it must have been something that came up suddenly."

Bob Anstruther said he heard what Anne was saying, though, that the group was not really doing enough to help people to know how to handle crises or to express them when they do feel them. What if there were people in the room tonight who were facing the same thing? Could they talk about it to the group?

Bill Duval said he could only speak for himself, but he for one had found what he was looking for in the group. He was looking for only one thing, and gradually he had discovered it.

It occurred to me that most of us do not know ourselves very deeply or consistently, and that important changes, like the one the Rittenhouses had just undergone, can come upon us so suddenly that we ourselves have had little forewarning.

Penny agreed. "We have our own private little worlds," she said, "where we have silly little thoughts and feelings we don't even tell to our husbands and wives. How could we possibly communicate them to the group?"

Bob pressed Bill. "I want to hear what it is Bill has found," he said.

"This will sound shallow to some of you," said Bill, "but I didn't know much about God, and I thought most of you were a lot more knowledgeable than I was. So I thought that if I just sort of hung around you, I would get to know him better, and I have."

Penny giggled nervously. "We're not very sophisticated Christians," she said.

"Come off it," said Bob.

"We can't talk theology and things like that," said Bill.

"That's a game," said someone else.

Bob and Dan had a single concern, and spoke of it almost at the same time. "I know we've beat this horse a lot, and nobody probably wants to drag it out again," said Dan, "but I hear us saying, or implying, that we're nervous again about having no structure."

A feeling of consent passed around the room.

I took a stab at an answer.

"It seems to me," I said, "that we have felt more excited and satisfied too on the occasions when we have had real encounter in the group. We've been bored the past two or three times because no one has really exposed himself or taken any risk. We're reluctant to plan any continuing structure, lest the structure take us over. But what if we worked with some semi-structures that we planned from time to time?

"For example: A few weeks ago we had dinner with a couple of friends. After dinner, the wife suggested that we play a little game. Each of us was to write down on a slip of paper the name of a vegetable we thought was most like us, the name of a car we thought most like us, the name of a piece of clothing, etc. Then she mixed up the sheets and read the name of a vegetable from one. The rest of us tried to guess who had identified himself that way. When we finally guessed, the person had to say why he identified with the vegetable. Then the rest of us said what vegetable he reminded us of. And so on through the list.

"You see, the game was important because it gave us feedback. We not only risked something in explaining who we thought we were, or how we saw ourselves, we got a chance to see how our impression matched the impressions of others. We met ourselves a little better."

I wondered if we might not try some things like that game.

Maybe one week we could all agree, during the week, to do some incongruous or zany thing, like wear a piece of ridiculous apparel in some public place, and then tell the group our reaction while we were doing it and the reaction we felt from others. It would expose us to the group in new and unexpected ways. Encounter would occur because there would be surprise.

It was readily agreed that we would try the vegetable game at our next meeting. Bill Duval said he was ready right then. Marnie Jones said she knew where she could get a simulated hunger game we could play some Thursday night.

We broke up feeling regretful for the Rittenhouses' pain but hopeful for the future of the group. I think a lot of us have begun to wonder how much longer this particular formation of a group will last. Maybe this will keep us going for a while.

We had prayer for the Rittenhouses. Dan Quillian said about all that could be said when he began. I thought it was unusually apt, and wished that ministers could pray as well—just asking God very simply and directly for all that any one could ask for the Rittenhouses at that particular time. Two or three others prayed briefly and Dan concluded.

Anne wondered afterwards how the Rittenhouses would have felt if they had known we were praying for them. She didn't think Eve was comfortable with prayer. I don't know. I have a hunch they would have wept.

Looking back, I cannot doubt that our failure to anticipate the Rittenhouses' separation, while salved by John's letter indicating that he himself had not expected it, was symptomatic of a more general failure with all those who attended our meetings. We were simply not adept enough at listening for the telltale clues to

people's deeper problems, or at structuring our exchanges in ways designed to elicit clues.

Listening is a fine art. Being a fine art, it is also very
difficult. Most of us are extremely inefficient at it. We
hear only a very narrow range of the signals actually
being transmitted by another individual at any, given
moment. Usually we focus on the content of the conversation—on the ideas or statements being exchanged
—and miss a wealth of nonverbal information being sent
out in such disguised forms as body posture, movement
or gesture, tone of voice, rate of speech, change in in-
flection, and even the degree of glibness or reticence.

It would be helpful for any group, early in its career,
to make a conscious effort to study some practical guide
to the communication process, including both the
sending and receiving of messages, and to receive basic
instructions from a competent psychologist or group
therapist about how to be attentive to the various levels
of interpersonal communication.

My own little study book, **To Meet—To Touch—To
Know,** begun after this experience with the Ritten-
houses and the sharing group, contains chapters on
"Common Barriers to Communication" and "Creative
Listening." It is available in an inexpensive edition from
the Methodist Publishing House (Nashville, Tenn.).

In the first of these two chapters, I suggest that one
of the most inhibiting factors in communication is the
fear which most people have of being criticized or rejected if they say what they are truly feeling or thinking.
The rule of social expediency—what I **think** you expect
me to say—governs most of our actual speech.

It is like the Charles Schulz comic strip "Peanuts"
in which Lucy says that if we use our imaginations we
can see a lot of things in the cloud formations. She
asks Linus what he sees. He replies that the clouds look
to him like the profile of the famous painter and
sculptor Thomas Eakins . . . and another group of clouds

reminds him of the stoning of the New Testament character Stephen. "Uh huh," says Lucy, "that's very good." Then she asks Charlie Brown what he sees. Charlie says, "Well, I was going to say I saw a ducky and a horsie, but I changed my mind!" Charlie was so intimidated by Linus's erudite imaginings that he dared not go into detail about his own homespun reactions.

Once you are conscious of this repression principle at work in a group, you realize that it is operative most of the time. Only rarely did our group seem to transcend it. Those times were the occasions when passions were released and people said things they would not normally say in a group. One of the things I observed about these times was that some people who were normally restrained began to use four-letter words in their remarks. You could tell then that their customary self-censorship was relaxed and they were disclosing more of their real feelings than they usually did.

One of the things Eve Rittenhouse, with her background in encounter sessions, had brought to our meetings was a way of cutting through the smoke screens we sent up and probing the persons behind them. She was a much more skilled and efficient technician in communication than the rest of us were. Most of us were somewhat threatened by this—there were times when Eve seemed almost surgical in her manner of getting at the truth—but we respected her immensely and knew that we always profited from her presence.

I have tried in the chapter on "Creative Listening" in the study book to suggest simple techniques which we can all employ to do a better job of listening to what others are really saying. They apply to all of our interpersonal relationships, to communication within the family as well as within the group or in business organizations. Some of the techniques are:

(1) Listen to everything the other person is transmitting, not merely what you are interested in or want to

hear. This includes nonverbal as well as verbal communications. Practice hearing and seeing everything. We are far too slovenly or inert in our reception of what others are broadcasting, and usually edit their material severely without really being aware of it, disposing of vitally important clues.

(2) Listen especially where you think you have heard or understood the other person. It is often precisely in the areas where we think we know others best that we miss the biggest clues. We stereotype the persons we know—pigeonhole them and categorize them—and then assume that we know how they think on almost any subject. Parents are especially prone to treat children in this manner. So are teachers. But we do it to almost every person we have frequent contact with.

Try to empty your mind and forget you have met the person before; pretend you are encountering him for the first time. Now what is he actually trying to communicate? You will be amazed at how much information you have neglected from the persons you thought you knew intimately.

(3) Now pick up on the new clues you have received. Ask the person to elaborate on certain remarks he has made. Probe with honest, helpful questions at the points of concern. Encourage a fuller revelation. Try entering as fully as you can into the other person's situation as he shares with you.

Psychologists have experimented in recent years with a technique called "doubling," in which two persons exchange roles and act out how they think they would feel if they were really in each other's situation. You can practice this without involving the other person at all—imagine you are in his shoes and how he sees the world from there.

One of the things we needed in our group but hadn't the foresight to design was some kind of "feedback" system. We doubtless missed a lot on nearly every occasion by not having some efficient technique of salvaging and playing back important hints, comments, and personal clues dropped during the course of the evening. The National Training Laboratories at Bethel, Maine, which have pioneered many of the group techniques now widely used in this country, have advocated the use of an "Observer" in group sessions. The observer's job is to refrain from participation in the interaction among the persons present and to function as a sensitive recorder. His observations are requested at some point in the session, often midway or nearly at the end of the period. If he is a good observer, he will review what has taken place in such a way as to point out where a profitable road was missed when somebody said something that was passed over too quickly, or where somebody seemed particularly agitated, or where a silence was especially eloquent, or where the whole group "copped out" by jabbering about some easy subject instead of facing the implications of a discovery already half-made or half-realized. He is a catalyst, in other words, to provoke reactions at points which the group either missed or tried to avoid. Such a catalytic agent can be especially helpful in a sharing group such as the one we had—only we didn't know it at the time.

The matter of the Rittenhouses' separation was not allowed to rest. Karla Marston, who felt especially close to them, made a move during the week. She called a meeting of ten wives to talk about what the church could be doing to help married couples and families be more sensitive to each other, and generally, in the day and age in which we live, to succeed at interpersonal relationships. Numerous suggestions were discussed, and another meeting scheduled in two weeks.

Several things finally resulted from this beginning, and two or three of them have had a significant impact on the church program. One is a "Mother's Day Out" arrangement to care for preschool children between the hours of nine and three. It was recognized that one of the "pressure areas" for young married persons is the prolonged confinement of parenthood when there are no relatives or close friends to share in the responsibilities of constant care for babies and infants. Now the church operates a nursery three days a week, staffed with professional and volunteer workers, where young mothers may leave their children at a very minimal expense.

Another outgrowth of the initial "meeting of concern" has been a volunteer round-robin dinner association in the church. Realizing that the pastoral care of church members by other members is usually relaxed or nonexistent in today's churches, where membership is highly mobile, transitory and scattered, the women decided that something should be done to introduce couples to one another on a more systematic and intimate basis than we had formerly had. Therefore they designed a dinner arrangement whereby many groups of four or five couples would gather in homes for dinner each month. By rotating the membership roll, each couple would be with a different group of people each month. Host couples would provide meat, starchy vegetable, and drink, and other couples would bring other items as indicated on the master sheet. Two single persons would constitute a "couple" for the purpose of integrating them into the list, and these singles-couples would shift continuously to provide as much exchange as possible among the singles.

We played the "vegetable game" Thursday night, only

without vegetables. Each person was asked to say which tree, which color, and which animal he identified with. "What you feel like—what you would probably be if you existed in that category instead of as a human being."

Here is a list of those who were present and their self-images:

Name	Tree	Color	Animal
Rachel Anstruther	willow	red	dog
Bob Anstruther	pine	green	dog
Liz Delacorte	wild cherry	royal blue	white rabbit
Mindy Carson	redbud	green	kitten
Bill Duval	sycamore	brown	chameleon
Penny Duval	maple	gold	mule
Marnie Jones	cedar	orange	Irish setter
Barney Hopkins	chinaberry	blue	gorilla
Dot Hopkins	oak	red	dog
Anne Killinger	willow	red	lioness
John Killinger	cypress	violet-red	mountain lion
Gretchen Wilder	wild plum	red	ibex
Libby Wheeler	cedar	blue	
Adele Hofman	pinon pine	blue	black bear
Helen Roos	maple	gold & green	rabbit
Ellen Harris	poplar	red-purple	giraffe
Judy Quillian	magnolia	yellow	opossum
Dan Quillian	oak	yellow	chameleon

The group had a lot of fun—even two or three of the men who expressed reluctance to engage in such "silliness" at first. Time passed quickly, and there was intense interest during the whole evening.

Feedback to individuals was minimal and almost invariably positive. Only three or four times did the group take exception to someone's self-image and actually try to correct it.

These occasions, as I recall them, were Rachel Anstruther's self-image as a willow tree ("because I bend in the wind, am easily swayed, irresolute, etc."); Bill Duval's picture of himself as a chameleon ("I adapt easily in any kind of crowd and don't have a strong personality of my own"); and Penny Duval's self-conception as a maple ("I just like them") and as a mule ("I have always worked hard and think I am really made for service").

I thought Rachel was much more resolute than she regarded herself as being. Two or three persons did not like Bill's use of a negative figure. Bill objected to Penny's self-characterization as a maple tree, saying he saw her as a birch. This was much approved by the group, as she is a slender, soft-spoken blonde and has a special, elegant character. And most of the group objected to her self-image as a mule, feeling that the mule was too ugly a beast for her. Ellen Harris said she ought to be a fawn or an antelope, and the group applauded this suggestion.

Several self-revelations were both informative and pathetic. Ellen's that she felt like a poplar tree and a giraffe, for instance, because she had always been tall and had a long neck. Barney's that he was a gorilla, an interesting beast, short, hairy, prone to breast beating, ugly, yet basically likeable. Bill and Dan's that they were chameleons, taking the color of their surroundings. And Judy's, that she felt like an opossum, "for no very good reason." Actually, she had a very good reason. She was very quiet during the evening, appeared to be withdrawing, and seemed to feel some tension with Dan, who occasionally appears to dominate her.

Among the most precise and revealing disclosures, I thought, were Adele Hofman's and Liz Delacorte's. Adele said she was a piñon pine, like those growing in New Mexico, because she liked to see herself standing tall and green against an azure New Mexico sky; and that she was a grizzly bear because she was playful when she was "out" and yet would withdraw or hibernate for long periods. In further describing the pine, she said that the piñon variety of pine has little flower-like cones all over it, and she feels like that— "as if I have little secrets hidden all over me."

Liz was noticeably specific about each of the categories, defining her choice in each case with a qualifying word— "wild cherry," "royal blue," "white rabbit." The wild cherry she identified with because of the wildness. And then, after explaining that she once had a white car that was known as The White Rabbit, she added that the rabbit ought to be regarded as wild, not tame, for she felt that she had a wild streak in her.

Perhaps the most comfortable images were Bill's sycamore tree, which is plain and identified with the farm, and Bob's pine tree and green color, both of which suggest restfulness, Arkansas hillsides (where Bob is from), and seem very appropriate to Bob's quiet, folksy character.

Among the most aesthetic self-concepts were Gretchen Wilder's wild plum ("short and round, like me, but with an exotic color") and ibex ("very sweet meat, a delicacy"), and Adele Hofman's piñon pine, seen against the blue sky.

And the most beautiful self-images, to me, were Anne's. She was a willow, she said, "because I have a lot of roots and need a lot of nourishment—drawing it from all of you— but then I give a lot too, and my arms are out, like willow limbs, returning what I take." "My color is red," she explained, "because I am very passionate. I rush into things— and people—without thinking, without warning, and then sometimes have to pull off." And the lioness, she said, was because she guarded her cubs ferociously and yet looked up to her male; very domestic, yet living apart from a lot of the animals.

The important thing about the evening was that everyone

participated, and, even in code, told something about his innermost feelings of who he was and how he related to the world around him. We were all amazed at some of the things we learned about each other. Several said that it was the most positive time we had had together.

9

I have been neglecting my journal—probably because I have felt that the last two or three meetings have not been noteworthy. At the one following the last I described, we tried a variation of the same approach. We wrote our names on slips of paper, placed them in a basket, and shuffled them. Then each of us drew out a slip, wrote on it a brief description of the person whose name was there, and put it back. A leader read the descriptions and we tried to guess the names. Somehow there was less enthusiasm for this than for the game the preceding Thursday night.

By prior agreement, the next Thursday night was given to role playing. Marnie Jones authored several situations—a mother trying to persuade her three-year-old daughter to come out of the locked bathroom, an American woman trying to explain to a French taxi driver that she wanted some Pepto Bismol, the president of Women of the Church informing the minister that the WOC wished to convert the church parking lot into a tennis court, a teenage girl justifying to her parents her desire to join a commune, and so on—and we took unlikely parts and played them out. The group was small. The men, in particular, had appeared to avoid the gathering.

The following week Anne and I were absent. I was in Atlanta on business, and Anne wanted to stay home with the children.

One of the members called Anne on Friday and told her that it had been a wonderful evening. The dozen persons present had discussed the Twenty-Third Psalm, a house for teenagers in Nashville where the kids read scripture constantly, listen to rock music, and give their testimonies. This had led to a resolution on their parts to have a more disciplined spiritual life, especially regarding prayer and Bible reading. They agreed to study the first eight chapters of Romans during the coming week, and at the next gathering to talk about what they had felt.

The person relating this to Anne commented, perhaps not unkindly, that the remarkable spirit they had felt occurred on a night when none of the three ordained clergymen and their wives were present, and that it might not have happened had they been there.

Apparently Bob and Rachel Anstruther had heard a similar report. Bob expressed to me on Sunday his concern about this feeling. I think we both felt awkward about the approaching Thursday evening. Should we go and possibly be a barrier to some who wanted an experience we seemed to be forbidding? Should we absent ourselves and cause some persons to think we didn't want to be there?

I saw Bob again on Thursday. We agreed that we couldn't stay away. We only regretted that there seemed to be some resentment of our presence.

The evening started in the usual way, with everyone visiting and chatting. Then Dan Quillian clapped his hands and called for order. Assuming the role of spokesman, he began talking about his attempts to read Romans and how he felt about it during the week. None of the participants said that it had been an unusually beneficial experience, but each still confessed to the need for self-discipline.

The group soon polarized much as some of us had feared it might, with one half seeming to argue for the importance of disciplined prayer and Bible study and the other half appearing to feel that what we needed was no routinized religion but more joy and spontaneity.

Ellen Harris, who had with her a copy of Keith Miller's **The Taste of New Wine,** referred to a passage in it where Miller appeared to castigate "scholastic" religion in favor of real, down-to-earth religious experience. This seemed to endorse a simple form of Bible reading and prayer. She, Dan Quillian, Adele Hofman and perhaps others felt that genuine "confrontation with Christ" occurred in this manner.

Rachel Anstruther, on the other hand, said that she didn't get anything from the scriptures that way. She needed to read several versions and a commentary or two, and then the whole thing seemed to come alive to her. Anne said that she didn't pray that way either. She never felt very far from God at any time, and did not need to "keep the lines of communication open," as Dan Quillian put it.

Gretchen Wilder confessed that she had given up regular formal prayer when she was twelve years old and rebelled against her family's prayer time. But she still prayed in diffuse ways every day, and occasionally went into a chapel to pray in a crisis. She listened carefully to pastoral prayers on Sunday too, she said, and meditated on the phrasing and suggestions during the week to come.

Jim Kenan, a medical doctor who had begun attending the sessions two or three weeks earlier, suggested that we practice a form of devotion together right then that the

Quakers used, namely silence. He felt that ten minutes of silence and meditation would be good for us.

Two or three evidently opposed this, though not in any sense bitterly, and continued to talk for a minute. But eventually the sound died out and we heard only the noises of automobiles on the street outside, a toilet flushing somewhere in the building, and our own breathing. I thought of John Cage's recording **4' 33"**, which is three movements of silence, allowing only for the external noises to become apparent.

To me, it was a restful time. I had had a trying week, and felt physically exhausted. I relished the chance to be quiet and to think. I felt as I often do when walking on a quiet afternoon, and restoration began to creep over me. Anne reached over and took my hand. I could tell she had been studying my face for two or three minutes. We smiled at each other. I looked around. There seemed to be tension on many faces. Only a couple of persons did not avert their faces when I looked into their eyes. I felt that there were many troubled souls there.

Jim finally broke the silence by talking about silence for a minute or two.

Musing on the effect of the period, I asked if anyone remembered Aldous Huxley's article in the old **Saturday Evening Post** series, "Adventures of the Mind." Huxley talked about the effect of physical conditioning on prayer and the visionary life. In Lent, he observed, many people in the Middle Ages were already suffering from protein deficiency; giving up certain foods during the period added to the deficiency. Consequently they were especially susceptible to hallucinative experiences. This was the dietary side of mystical visions.

Huxley also spoke of the effects of prolonged singing

or dancing on the brain. Deoxygenation results, producing a light-headedness and suggestability. I thought of revival meetings I had attended where the congregation was kept singing for forty-five minutes through a prolonged invitation to repentance; eventually some people always succumbed. I didn't draw any conclusions. I merely suggested that prayer is a very complicated matter, involving the body as well as the will and the mind and the heart.

A little later, Jim asked me a question about prayer and mature religious experience. I commented that I thought Gretchen's expression of her manner of prayer was very normal and healthy for her, and that the kind of thing reported to be occurring for the young people at the Twenty-Third Psalm was probably healthy for them. I said that I had gone through such an ecstatic period myself as a young man, and that now I felt more the way Gretchen did. Each way was appropriate in itself.

It did bother me, I confessed, to hear a group of lay renewal leaders recently at another church testifying to their religious experience the same way the kids at the Psalm would speak of it. They were doctors, lawyers, communications people, housewives, and so on—probably none under thirty. It seemed to me, I said, that unless they learned to relate their experience with Christ to the particularities of their daily living, they were condemned to having the same initial experience over and over again the rest of their lives, and that it would become harder and harder to generate enthusiasm for it. It was probably all right the first time—maybe even the second and third times. But then the experience would become a parody of itself, and then a parody of the parody and so on.

At this, Ellen Harris bolted up from where she had been sitting on the floor, said she couldn't stand it another minute, she was about to scream, where were her shoes, she was going to get out before she screamed, she didn't want us to hear her scream, she had to leave—and left.

It all happened too suddenly for anybody to say anything. After Ellen had gone, Judy Quillian said, "Somebody stop her. Somebody go tell her to come back. Sombody help her."

I was sitting next to Judy, and my reaction was quick: "Why?" I asked. "I can't personally say that I give a damn right now. If she feels that way, maybe she has to go."

I thought of the times when a child of mine has had to go to his room and be alone—I couldn't put my arms around him and charm him back—it would have violated his rights, his privacy, his genuine feelings.

Ellen's husband was still in the group. He didn't say anything. In a few minutes, he left.

Maybe, it was suggested, we were at a dividing point. In the beginning, there were those who wanted to divide into small groups, but the majority had said no. Now, maybe we were ready. Maybe we were operating at different levels, and would be comfortable with smaller groups in which the aims and directions were more unified.

Adele Hofman had to leave to take her babysitter home, and Helen Roos, who was riding with her, went too. It was obvious that we could not make a major decision about direction. We would have to wait until next week. So we all began to rise and prepared to leave.

Feelings had been strong—much stronger than most of us realized. Resentments, antipathies, anxieties, all sorts of emotional reactions were at work. I felt good that Ellen had exploded. Explosions often serve to clear the air. An open agenda is always easier to deal with than a closed one. Maybe things will pick up now. We'll wait and see.

10

This is where the diary ends. The group never got off the ground again. We met a few more times, and tried splitting up into predesignated groups, one oriented toward prayer and Bible study, the other toward encounter techniques. But it was over. Things just weren't the same any more. Those of us in the encounter type of group missed the Rittenhouses. We also missed the Harrises and Quillians and Hofmans, whose strong individualities had helped us all to know ourselves better.

Was the whole experiment a failure?

I don't think so. Even if it was, it is often possible to learn as much from failures as it is from successes, and we probably learned a lot from our experience.

On the purely pragmatic level, a number of things came out of our strivings.

First there were the new programs and structures within the church, such as the Mother's Day Out and the rotating dinner groups which I have mentioned. These have added a new dimension of human caring to the overall way in which the church operates. The caring proceeds at a functional level instead of a merely ideological level. And the incentive for these programs clearly derived from something dynamic within the group.

Then, near the end of the spring of the year in which the group disbanded, a Lay Renewal emphasis was held in the church. The group both was and wasn't responsible for this. Dick Hofman was actually the driving force behind the emphasis. He and Adele had wanted and talked about such an event for a long time. They might have worked up enough interest in other people to have gotten it off the ground without the group, but the group was definitely involved in the chemistry of what happened. For one thing, it gave Dick a forum for talking up Lay Renewal. For another, it fed a hunger which other persons in the group had for something like a Lay Renewal movement within the entire fellowship of the church. And perhaps most significantly of all, it provided the Renewal meetings, when they did come, with a nucleus of persons already accustomed to the level of personal sharing of feelings and beliefs which is one of the primary aims of Lay Renewal.

The Renewal, by almost anybody's measuring stick, was a success in the life of the church. Large percentages of the membership turned out on Friday night for a family dinner and sharing session, on Saturday for both daytime and nighttime sessions and dinner on the grounds, and on Sunday for both an informal "worship in the round" at an early hour and the more formal experience of worship at the regular hour. Nearly everyone seemed to participate with ease. The elderly joined as openly in the confessional times as the young, and the usual lines of demarcation between groups of all sorts appeared to fade away. The church wasn't "carried away" by the experience; but everyone felt that it was a warm and meaningful event whose incandescence would continue to glow in the life of the congregation long after it was over.

Out of the Renewal itself three new groups were formally initiated in the church—one study group and two Yoke-fellows groups—all of which are still functioning at the time of this writing. One Yokefellows group is designed to give more importance to the discipline of prayer and Bible reading, and the other gives clear precedence to an encounter type of emphasis, thus conforming more or less to the eventual styles of our proto-group. The participants in both Yokefellows groups agreed at the outset to pay a fee and take the battery of personality tests known as the Minnesota Multiphasic exam. Each person's responses to the test are programmed through a computer, and details of personality analysis plus suggested reading assignments are submitted to the individual periodically. The details of analysis frequently become the basis for discussion within the groups, so that an element of personal encounter is maintained constantly during the groups' existences.

Reaction to the new groups is mixed. A few persons speak nostalgically of the old initial group, and feel that basically it accomplished all that has been accomplished for them. Others, and I would guess a majority, feel that the groups are now achieving what the initial group wanted to achieve but did not.

The semiprofessional leadership team which came to the church for the Lay Renewal session, it ought to be said, laughed when our initial group attempt was described and they were told that we had between eighteen and twenty-five persons at each meeting. They could not imagine that anything profitable could emerge in a group that large.

Still another long-range effect of the group's efforts is more difficult to lay a finger on because it is diffused throughout the life and worship of the church. It has to do with a new degree of warmth and humanity in the tone of the church's life. As a professional sermon critic, I have noticed it in Barney Hopkins's preaching. He doesn't talk any less about God than he did, but I sense a new concern for the relationship of God to the particularities of the human situation—to human loneliness, confusion, despair, poverty, bitterness, resentment, jealousy, inadequacy, fear, and brokenness.

The same thing is true of the patterns of worship. Take this little excerpt from the Call to Worship on a recent Sunday morning, for example:

> Pastor: Who are you who gather here?
> People: *We are human beings whom God has made.*
> Pastor: In what spirit do you come?
> People: *We come seeking peace, because our lives are fragmented; we come seeking forgiveness, for we are sinners; we come seeking love, because we are lonely.*

There is an air of personal reality about those words. People don't leave their humanity at the door when they come in; they bring it into the pews with them, they speak of it and sing of it, they lay it at the altar with their offerings. The Communion is not an empty ritual full of the rhetoric of church tradition and nothing else; their private suppers of pain and passion are mingled with the pain and passion of Christ; they verbally bless their neighbors as they hand the bread and juice to them in the pew.

That is another thing. I used to be a purist about the sacraments. It bothered me that the church was always talking about the bread and the wine, and yet, because of the Temperance League mentality of church people in America, served bread and grape juice. It seemed hypocritical to me, like a lot of things we do in church.

But last Sunday our family sat with Liz Delacorte in church. Liz, it will be recalled, is an alcoholic. It suddenly occurred to me how stupid I had been. If real wine were used in the

Communion, Liz could not partake of it—not even from one of those diminutive glasses in the silver Swiss-cheese platters they are served from. And how many alcoholics are there in churches around the world on any given Sunday? What a fool I had been! No congregation could afford to take a chance on excluding a single worshiper from this fellowship meal. From now on I shall gladly have grape juice instead of wine.

Thus the human dimension of things gets reinvested from the group's association and insights back into the worship and life of the church itself. This is only one instance. There are countless times when it happens. The total effect of the group's six months or so together cannot be measured in a mere statement of whether the group "failed" or "succeeded." It can only be described as an ongoing process, like a stone that fell in the water and continues to send out little ripples long after it has sunk from view. I expect, in my own life, to be seeing the ripples many years from now. They will be less frequent then, and probably smaller. But I am confident of seeing them.

When all is said and done, what did we learn from the experience of the group? What insights are worth bracketing or underlining for others who are now engaged in group encounters or will undertake such encounters in the future? Maybe a simple listing will be helpful.

(1) The need for small groups in people's lives today is simply staggering and inestimable.

Our society is the most rootless, mobile, anonymous society man has ever known. The old units of interrelationship such as township, neighborhood, school, work, and family have in most cases dissolved into shifting, impersonal, amorphous nearnesses or propinquities and little more. We are all so isolated and alone that we think we are becoming a little crazy; we lack feedback on who we are and how we appear to the world around us; our only references are internal ones.

There are plenty of secondary and tertiary groups to keep us active; most of us, in fact, feel that we are far too active. But our desperate need is for primary groups—small associations of persons who are committed to the group they are in and the persons who are in it with them, so committed that their lives get all entangled and they provide a constant feedback to each other's words, looks, and deeds.

If the church is to meet human need at a fundamental level in our time, it must begin by redeveloping the primary group which is so absent from the scene. It cannot assume that it is already a primary group. The truth is that it is as much debilitated by the modern disease of impersonalism as any other structure left over from better days.

(2) The first thing the small group accomplishes is to get people to take off their masks with each other.

This usually happens, but it does not happen easily. Most of us are extremely reluctant to let our masks go. We are secretly afraid that others will not like our real selves, so we develop elaborate masks and costumes and scripts to seem like somebody else.

We rationalize to ourselves by saying that we don't really trust others enough to disclose our inner feelings to them. The truth is that we don't trust ourselves enough to be sure that others will respond positively to us when we aren't play-acting. Therefore we expend more energy trying to make our imaginary selves or projected selves attractive than we do to make our real selves attractive.

As Fritz Perls says, "Most people only live for their image. Where some people have a self, most people have a void, because they are so busy projecting themselves as this or that."

(3) The group helps us to do what we can seldom do alone

because it provides a climate of acceptance in which it is easier to unmask and because it finally demands a certain amount of unmasking before it can interact with us.
We begin to realize that the group responds positively and affirmatively to other people when they let their masks slip. At some point we may even become ecstatic at the realization that the finest relationships in the group are built not on the strengths of the individuals involved, but on their weaknesses. We are encouraged to "test the waters" ourselves— to drag out old feelings of hostility and resentment, of failure and inadequacy, of frustration and longing—and we feel good when nobody is shocked or alienated by what we say. Instead, we find that they have a new freedom to relate to us as persons.

They feel that they know us at last, that they are "into" us, that they have something solid and particular to relate to. Our confessions of inner feelings become points of contact with which they can identify similar feelings. Then, when we hear their explanations that they have experienced the same things we have, we suddenly realize that we weren't different from them after all. We didn't have to hide our true selves. We can begin to deal with them from our real centers, from who we really are, instead of from those false centers we were always projecting to fool other people.

Most people are amazed, at this point, to discover how much more energy they have for living; they aren't pouring all of it into the maintenance of disguises and subterfuges.

(4) **The group can be trusted to do this.**
That is important, that it can be trusted.

Carl Rogers, the eminent psychological counselor, says in his book **Carl Rogers on Encounter Groups** that it took him many years to come to this realization, but now he is firmly convinced of the truth of it. Almost every group he has ever worked with, he says, functions "like an organism"; it seeks out the areas in itself where there is most falsity and disease, and goes to work on those areas to restore them to health. Just as the human body sends antibodies to fight areas of infection in itself, the group directs healing attention toward individuals within it who need it most.

Only twice in all his experience, says Dr. Rogers, has he known of negative results which occurred as a result of group encounters; in both cases, potentially psychotic persons had later to receive professional treatment for their conditions.

(5) Once we have experienced the group's acceptance of who we really are without our disguises, we are able to accept ourselves more fully and to feel less insecure in all our relationships.

Then actual change in attitudes and behavior begins to occur. Scientifically conducted studies of numerous groups have verified this.

The basic hindrance to change in persons and in groups is a sense of uncertainty or insecurity. Once the person feels comfortable with himself and the degree of acceptance he is receiving from other persons, he becomes free enough from constrictive anxieties to release himself from a particular role and move toward new positions.

As Dr. Maxwell Maltz says in **Psycho-Cybernetics,** "The 'self-image' is the key to human personality and human behavior. Change the self-image and you change the personality and the behavior." A plastic surgeon, Dr. Maltz cites cases in which the transformations of people's physical appearances have notably affected their manners of relating to the world around them.

A similar pattern is discernible in encounter groups: people's self-images are altered by the feedback they get from the group, then their ways of relating and behaving are altered too.

(6) Obviously and significantly, these basic changes in the way people conceive of themselves and behave toward others carry over from the group meetings to other areas of their lives.

A person begins to get a new image of himself within the group and then tests that new image in the world outside the group. Generally he discovers that life in the larger world is easier and more enjoyable for him than it was before.

Occasionally he will be disappointed and will return to the group as to the womb, saying, "I wish other people were like you people." At this point it is important for the group to remind him that people are not really that different anywhere, and that he can seek strategies for drawing other persons in the larger world into the kind of relationship he has found in the group. The group must not become an escape mechanism or a substitute for a healthy method of relating to other persons generally.

More often than not, though, participants in group meetings of the kind I have described find that their manner of relating to most other people in their lives has become improved. Parents have more patience with their children, husbands and wives are more open and considerate with each other, businessmen are more sensitive to the personalities of their bosses or employees, teachers get along better with their students, and ministers feel more comfortable with their congregations.

(7) Because reinforcement of what a person is learning in his group is usually necessary, it is important that the group experience have some continuity about it.

While short, intensive sessions such as the weekend marathons are helpful, many therapists believe that there needs to be some kind of extended support for reinforcing the insights gained in them. The intensive sessions retain their significance as reference points, but they gradually slip away unless something is done to help the person retain their benefits.

We probably fumbled the ball in our group by not having a marathon session at one point along the way. We discussed the possibility of a weekend retreat together, but numerous difficulties surfaced in each discussion and the idea was never carried out. Looking back, I think that this intensive experience might have saved us, might have been a turning point, in those weeks when we were beginning to flounder and drift apart.

But if one were to choose between an intensive experience and a less intense but more sustained one, the latter is probably better. The loneliness which many people feel when they first join a group can sometimes come back more severely than ever after a brief alleviation such as the marathon group is likely to provide; alienation or rejection is experienced at a new level.

The church is in a highly favorable position at this point. It can sustain group possibilities for people on a more or less permanent basis, so that they need never be without some opportunity for sharing.

(8) It is important that groups be provided with trained leaders who are competent at facilitating interaction.

I was first opposed to this idea, and, though I never spoke against it openly, was secretly glad that our group never got around to bringing in an outsider to act as a catalyst. Frankly, I was afraid that this "outsider" would try to manipulate us, and I shy instinctively from the slightest hint of manipulation. But I think I am wiser about the matter now. I see that some of the persons in our group experienced "rejection at a new level" even though the group continued to meet. A good facilitator would have caught this and reintroduced the needs of these persons until others in the group recognized the same thing and did something about it. A skilled leader has trained himself to observe many things that most of us miss in a human scene. To use Theodore Reik's term, he listens with "the third ear." If he does attempt to manipulate others, the group will not hesitate to tell him this; he is as subject to correction as anyone else in the group, or maybe more so. But a good facilitator has been through the mill many times as a person, and knows his own personality deficiencies. He tries to keep these within bounds in order to be as transparent as possible to the needs of the group he is helping.

I find it deplorable, as a seminary professor, that seminaries have done so little to provide adequate training for group facilitators. Surely priorities have got to be rethought and more provision made at this point.

Churches, by the same token, will have to reconsider the significance of group leadership in their staffing arrangements. Present staff members can be given brief leaves of absence to participate in learning sessions at such places as the National Training Laboratories and the Esalen Institute in Southern California, and persons with leadership qualifications can be sought in replacing present staff personnel or designing new situations for expanded ministry. Most pastors and church workers, brought along under an earlier, hierarchical conception of interpersonal organization, are totally inept at the methods necessary for small group leadership. Their models of leadership, however useful in other ways and other places, can be stifling and harmful here.

(9) Groups should be small enough to permit active participation by all persons present.

Most experienced therapists suggest eight or ten as an

optimal number, with the advantages diminishing on either side of those figures.

This was another place where our group fumbled the ball. We simply didn't know any better, or, if we did, we were reluctant to subdivide and miss out on intimately knowing any of those who would not be in our particular group. If we had been smaller, the rate of exchange might have been greater. Several persons who rarely spoke or reacted to what was happening would have been drawn into the game more fully. The sense of true intimacy would have been heightened considerably, and we would not have the feeling now that we left many stones unturned and many appeals for recognition unheard.

(10) There is maximal advantage to minimal structure.

Groups develop their own agenda if left to do so. The most pressing agenda has to do with the achievement of honest, free and open sharing, and, if there is no superficial agenda to divert the attention from this one, the group invariably finds ways of getting at it. Structures in most groups are means of avoiding real confrontation between persons. Attention becomes fixated on programs, sequences, plans, actions, entertainments, etc. It may be that the distinctive feature of the small group we are talking about is its non-structure, its actual resistance to the usual structure, so that persons are finally forced to consider each other as the subject matter of the time spent together.

To be sure, most people are extremely nervous at first in a group which has no structure. They have an oppressive sense of "wasted" time. They are anxious to set rules, establish definitions, get down to cases, and all the other busy things we do when we are in the company of others.

But, as becomes apparent, wasting time with others is a necessary ingredient to real self-discovery. Until I stop struggling and cease fidgeting and forget about my appointments, I am giving precedence to my role, to who I am as life has been organized for me. When I relax, letting time and performance go, my inner self has a chance to compose itself. I can begin to act and react as I really am, not as the person dictated to me by my circumstances in life.

The flow of time is meaningless to a child, and it is likewise meaningless to an adult who is engaged in play or pleasurable activity. We begin to get back to who we were as children—and are—when we psychologically throw away the clock.

(11) Recovering the self means recovering the body as well as the mind.

Most of us over thirty grew up in a culture which taught us that the body was either evil or tended to get us in trouble. Consequently we learned to communicate more and more with our mouths and less and less with the remainder of our bodies. We repressed the body as a means of communication.

Now psychologists tell us that this is unnatural and that we are at least slightly schizophrenic because of it. A healthy person is an interacting unit of mind and body. He expresses himself freely in the way he moves and in the ease with which he regards his own body and touches the bodies of others.

I have already observed that there was a noticeable change in posture among the participants of our sharing group whenever feelings became particularly intense. Sometimes it was signaled by people's moving to sit on the floor instead of in chairs. Often it resulted in somebody's reaching out to touch somebody else, or in a kiss or an embrace. The more relaxed we became as persons, the less guarded we tried to be, the more easily we related at a physical level.

Clothes are an expression of body attitude too, and the manner of dress in the group is significant. As Charles Reich points out in **The Greening of America,** most people change clothes as they change roles, wearing one outfit for work, another for play, and another for sleep. The youth culture, he contends, opposes this divided nature of man, and so adopts a form of highly casual dress for all activities.

The only occasions when people in our group came dressed up were when they had come in from other activities and had not had time to change; normally our dress ran from casual to extremely casual. Two of the men felt so comfortable in houseshoes that they occasionally wore houseshoes to the group. Many people took their shoes off during a session. There is a correlation between physical comfort and psychological relaxation or openness. Most people reveal themselves to one another more readily on a fishing trip or at a ball game than they do in a church where all the men wear ties and the women wear girdles and tight-fitting shoes. I think it was a mark of the influence of our group when some of the women began to attend meetings at the church in everyday dresses, skirts and sweaters, and even in slacks.

What does it say about the church when we acknowledge that it is one of the places in our society where people wear their finest clothes and appear as their most perfumed and immaculate selves?

(12) The kind of interaction which occurs in small groups is extremely important in the overall life of the church.

As an institution, the church is as much a victim of the communication boondoggle as any other organization. It may be even more of a victim, because it often assumes that it automatically achieves communion and communication by virtue of the fact that it is the church.

There is probably not a church anywhere that does not have within it numerous levels of understanding. People operate at various stages of sophistication regarding language, myth, history, scripture, etc. These levels or stages separate us from other church members unless they are consciously addressed and discussed, and unless we can arrive at a quality of personal relationship which keeps mere differences of opinion or understanding in the proper perspective. The small group functions to counteract the separation. It brings us together as persons and helps us to understand conflicting opinions in terms of their personal dimensions. The significance of this cannot be overstressed. Even ministers and leaders in the church cannot perform their responsibilities with sensitivity apart from the kind of interplay which is discovered in the group. I know that Barney Hopkins would bear me out on this. The minister who is not actively engaged in the group process with various types of persons in his congregation—the young and the elderly, the poor and the well-to-do, the simple and the complex, the academic and the barely literate, the repressed and the free—often misses the mark completely with these people. He assumes that he knows them when in fact he does not.

The group sensitizes us to other persons and their particular ways of thinking. It does not necessarily eliminate differences and homogenize opinions. But it sensitizes—it develops a feeling for them. And it is not an overstatement to say that there is no true communion in any church or organization until this has happened.

(13) Finally, people feel God in their lives when they feel good about their interpersonal relationships and the world they live in.

This is not to say that they don't feel him, or think they do, when they feel bad and all alone. But there is nothing more natural for a man, when things are going well for him and he feels a sense of buoyancy about life, than to identify his good feelings with God. The very words "God" and "good" are obviously related in their etymological origin.

There has been a lot of talk in recent years about the so-called "death" of God, as though he had either abdicated or was never around from the beginning. What this talk reflected more than anything else was the sense of emptiness in man himself. He didn't **feel** God any more. He didn't have any more sense of the transcendent or the holy in his affairs. He lost hope and faith in anything or anybody beyond the confusion and despair he was experiencing in the world. Instead of speaking accurately and saying, **"I** am dead," he projected his feelings onto his religion and said, **"God** is dead."

The fact or truth involved in all of this is that religion is essentially experiential in nature. That is, it consists primarily of what happens to us and how we make sense of that. To be sure, there is a historical side to it, and Christianity is also the record of what happened to some people a long time ago and how we make sense of that. But unless something is happening to us, something present and personal, we cannot go on permanently subsisting on the record of what happened to somebody else. If we are not convinced by the evidence from our own lives that God is in the world overcoming its brokenness and alienation, we gradually cease to believe that he was really in the world on those other occasions. We may continue to repeat the Apostles' Creed and say with our lips, "I believe in God the Father Almighty," but we don't actually mean it. We could more honestly agree with the writer of Ecclesiastes when he says, "Emptiness, emptiness, everything is empty."

One of the most vital discoveries we made in our weekly group was that when we felt healthy and good as persons we also felt a renewed sense of the presence of God in our lives. When we had really shared ourselves with others, laying bare our innermost feelings, and had experienced acceptance and affirmation from them, he became a living reality to us.

I don't think I'll ever forget the night John Rittenhouse,

who had known his own "dark night of the soul," testified that the affirmation of the group had made him feel so good all week that he had even begun to believe in heaven again. And I'll never forget some of the worship services I attended during the months our group was meeting. They were infused with a new sense of excitement and intensity—not because God was any different, but because we were. We were open to him because we were living in the overflow of the group experience.

11

This could go on and on—and would, if I didn't simply put a stop to it. The reader can perceive that I am no impartial observer. I have been stimulated and excited by what transpired in our group and am perhaps overly anxious to convey a sense of it to others in order that they might be encouraged to try the group experience themselves. As I said in the beginning, though, this is a very personal kind of diary. I have not tried to be entirely objective in reporting what I have seen and felt, but have allowed my feelings to surface whenever they displayed enough momentum to do so.

I also set down in the beginning a description of my personal state of mind at the time when I first became associated with the group. It seems in order, therefore, for me to conclude with some statement of what I perceive the experience to have done for me. What did I get from it? How did it affect my life in more or less permanent ways? What do I know about myself that I did not know before? Was it all worthwhile? Would I do it again?

In the first place, I have a clearer perspective of my loneliness. I know that Anne and I are not the only lonely people in the world. On the contrary, almost everybody is either lonely or has some lonely times in his life. Of course I knew this before. But that was at a **theoretical** level. Now I have a fresher experience of the loneliness of others. I have a new appreciation for the declaration of R. D. Laing that people can never experience other people's experience and become perfectly united to them in that way. Loneliness, isolation, distance—this is an inevitable facet of human existence for every one of us. Realizing this, I don't feel so tragic about my own sense of aloneness. Instead, I apply my energy to feeling and coping with the general tragedy of humanity.

At the same time, I have experienced a new sense of affirmation in my life. I have had some real feedback from a few of the people in the group. Once in a while they held the mirror up to me so that I got a more realistic picture of myself. I don't feel as crazy, senseless, or shadowy as I did. I have perceived in a new way where the outlines of my life are, how I strike other people, what my mode of being in the world is. In the language of a navigator, I have got a "fix" on my position. I'm not a lonely little dot traveling at high speed all over the ocean without any reference to any other dot. Now I know where a few other dots are, and it has given me a vital new feeling of self-confidence.

Because I do have a clearer understanding of how I am being received by others, I have an increased sense of freedom to speak openly of how I feel about most things. I feel less necessity to play the little games we invariably play when we are not comfortable in the presence of others. My most important contribution to a relationship, I have come to see, is myself, without any fencing around, any jockeying for position, or any polite deception.

This sounds simple to achieve, but it really isn't. The reason it isn't is that it isn't a matter of courage. Most of us have enough courage to be ourselves, especially if we believe it important. The real problem is in knowing who we are and how we really feel. Until we have a healthy sense of affirmation from others, we are not sure which feelings we have are truly ours and which are merely conditional on our living as alienated selves. We can be so sick from our alienation and loneliness that we don't trust ourselves to make any judgments about how we are actually responding to another person or situation. I was at this point. The reader will recall that I confessed to feeling sick. My world was so shot through with confusion and terror that I was seldom certain about my feelings. How could I rely on them? They were affected by so many things. I had a poor sense of reality. It seemed to come and go. I didn't know when to trust it and when not to.

Now I feel healthy again. The world isn't any simpler. It is still complicated. But at least it stands still in its complexity, and isn't buzzing around my head into new configurations all the time. I know who I am, the positive side as well as the negative. I am not puzzled any more by my own voice, wondering if it is the real me speaking or somebody else. I am able to speak honestly because I honestly think I know who I am. I project from the center of my being, not from any of a hundred points around the hazy circumference. I feel the pull of gravity there, concentrating me, defining me, giving me a particular existence with a particular set of dimensions.

It is a joyful thing. I am glad to be me. I am glad to know who I am. I am glad to be able to speak less guardedly, less equivocably, less tentatively. I am glad to take the responsibility for my life.

Taking this responsibility again, I see clearly one thing I have been totally blind to. I see that my spiritual growth was actually arrested in adolescence, over twenty years ago. All those intervening years have been devoted to the picture I had then of what it is to be a Christian and a minister. I had assumed during all that time that the church exists in a certain way, a certain pattern, and that my relationship to it would likewise take a certain form.

Thus, while I have been having many kinds of experience in the world, I have grievously wronged that experience by trying always to fit it into my preconceived patterns or expectations. I have not allowed it to teach me the important things it might have taught me, or to carry me away from the person I was to the person I might have become. What I have been living was not life but death. At least it was only a kind of suspended animation.

Now, thank God, I believe I am open again to the significance of my experience. I am willing to believe that my life, indeed, my whole world, can become something entirely other than what I had conceived of its being.

I am able, moreover, to place more and more importance in concrete religious deeds and relationships, and less and less in the vague generalities which I feel have so dominated my existence. I am ashamed of myself now for having spent so much of my life **thinking** about religion and so little of it in specific acts of helpfulness or comradeship. I tremble at the realization that I almost became a religious abstraction, that I almost lived my entire existence as an abstraction. I was like Camus' Monsieur Clamence in **The Fall:** I was sometimes most absent when I gave the appearance of being most present.

Now, for me, **people** are most clearly at the center of what it means to be religious. I stuff my earlier pieties and religiosity in a cocked hat, whatever that means. Christianity— not the institution that has become synonymous with it, but the way of Jesus—does not begin with rules and forms and programs. It begins with people. It is specific and it is relational. It occurs in the world, if it occurs, one step at a time.

And that step is the nearest one, the finite one, the one that can be taken from where we are at this very moment.

That's the long and the short of it. I am open to life again. This time it is in a way I have never been open before, because it is the first time I have ever accepted failure and begun from there.

It's funny, now that I say it, but that marks a turning point in my life. I never admitted before that I might fail. I didn't become what I intended to become, and I blamed it on a lot of external factors. They were there, to be sure, and they may have been to blame. That isn't the important thing. The important thing is that now it doesn't matter. Now I don't care. Now my life doesn't have to turn out a certain way. I failed to be what I meant to be, and I am honestly glad of it. I can thank God it didn't turn out according to my design, my little set of blueprints. If it had, my whole world would have been signed, sealed, and delivered according to my understandings as an adolescent. Now it explodes on all sides of me like a fantastic display of fireworks, illuminating skies I had never seen before. Maybe this is grace, and I have never been out of it. Anyway, I have never been more excited about life.

No more loneliness? I can't say that. It is too extravagant a thing to say. To be human is to be condemned to be lonely, at least part of the time.

But it is different now, for Anne as well as for me. We still feel it, but it isn't the same. Now we remember. We remember a base we touched on the way around—a particular tree we passed in the deep woods—a certain star that crossed the sky before us—and we know we are on course. We smile— it is a bittersweet memory—and we go on.

It is good to remember such things.

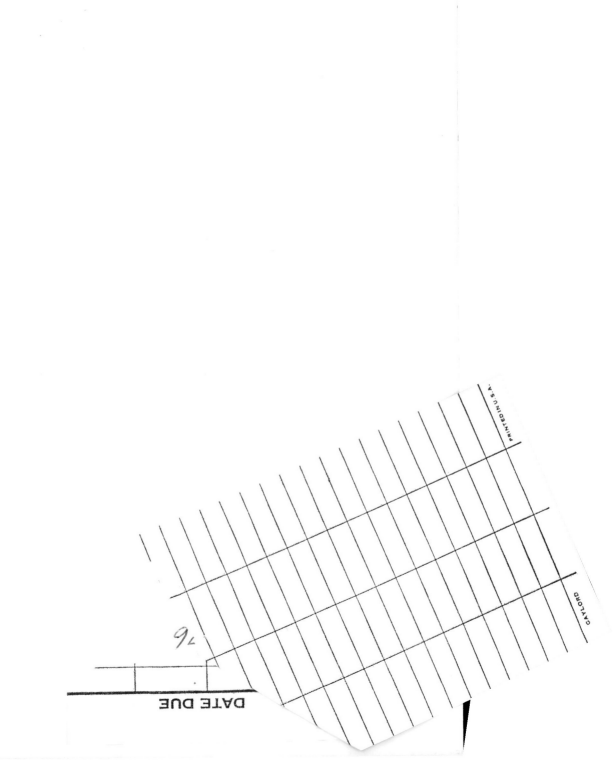